The Ambiguous Consensus

The
AMBIGUOUS
CONSENSUS

A Study of Local Government
in FRANCE

MARK KESSELMAN

Columbia University

ALFRED · A · KNOPF · NEW YORK

THIS IS A BORZOI BOOK,
PUBLISHED BY ALFRED A. KNOPF, INC.

FIRST PRINTING

Library of Congress Catalog Card Number: 67-20625
Manufactured in the United States of America.

To Wendy

PREFACE

❊ Most of the material for this study was gathered during doctoral research in France from 1962 through 1964. A Fulbright Fellowship in 1962–63 enabled me to conduct interviews with over fifty French municipal government officials in the provinces—mostly mayors, and also town clerks and municipal councilors in the Calvados and the Gironde. The interviews ranged from one to three hours in length and were relatively open, although within the general format of a questionnaire.[1]

Thanks to a Predoctoral Training Fellowship from the Social Science Research Council, I was able to conduct interviews in Paris during 1963–64 with legislators and administrators in the Ministry of the Interior, and also to obtain electoral data for the communes in three French departments: the Calvados, the Gironde, and the Nord.

While I have learned about French local political life from published accounts and statistical analysis, my major source of information has been discussions with French administrators and elected representatives. The Ministry of the Interior was extremely helpful; among the many administrators

[1] The questionnaire is reproduced in Appendix A.

there who facilitated my research, I would particularly like to thank Gabriel Pallez, Directeur Général des Collectivités Locales; and Alain le Taillandier de Gabory, Chef de Bureau des Affairs Politiques. Mayors and other officials interviewed were promised anonymity and therefore cannot be thanked by name; nor are their names cited in the text. I am, however, deeply grateful for their generous cooperation and for the care with which they introduced me to French local politics.

The apolitical style that will be described is especially prevalent in rural communes: this book is primarily a study of village government in France. And yet, despite wide differences in the characteristics of the communes and mayors studied, many of the findings converge. While the ambiguous consensus is associated above all with small-town politics, it affects local politics in large French cities as well.

Furthermore, my time is the present. Although the rivalry between M. *l'instituteur* Tafardel and M. *le curé* Ponosse had great relevance for the local politics of Clochemerle in 1923 (and the rivalry between the mayor and curé shaped 19th century local politics in Roger Thabault's village), it is remarkable how little past conflicts erupt into present-day French local politics. Looking to the future, Henri Mendras, Gordon Wright, Laurence Wylie and others have pointed to important changes at the local level in France.

This book, concerned with the present, may describe a waning phenomenon. I have attempted to portray a typical style in French local politics that continues to be influential, and my purpose has not been to predict its future. However, the strength of the prevalent style that will be described should not be underestimated. Rather than recent innovations producing a rupture with tradition, local leaders may well find a way to assimilate change without destroying current practice.

I have benefited from a great deal of thoughtful and valuable assistance. I would like to express my gratitude to Michel Crozier, Georges Dupeux, Henry W. Ehrmann, M. M. Goldsmith, Bernard Gournay, the late Morton Grodzins, Stanley Hoffmann, the late Otto Kirchheimer, Nathan Leites, Grant McConnell, Duncan MacRae, Jr., Marcel Merle, Jean-Pierre Worms, and Laurence Wylie.

Grateful acknowledgment is made to the Columbia University Council for Research in the Social Sciences for a summer grant in 1965 which permitted me to prepare my manuscript for publication; and also to the European Institute of Columbia University's School of International Affairs for a research grant in 1966 which made it possible to examine recent material in France bearing on my study. I would like to thank research assistants: John E. Fiske III, Daniel Kleinman, and Martin Pomp.

Portions of the Introduction and most of Chapter I have already appeared in the *American Political Science Review* (December 1966), whose permission to reprint is gratefully acknowledged.

My wife demonstrated rare talent as a political scientist on two continents.

New York   **Mark Kesselman**
January 1967

CONTENTS

The Ambiguous Consensus

INTRODUCTION

Beneath the turbulence of French national politics, there has been an unbroken practice of local government in France for centuries. During the Great Revolution, France's 44,000 religious parishes were transformed into communes—the fundamental unit of civil government in France.[1] Since then, the number of French communes and the structure of local government have remained largely the same. French communes are governed by a popularly elected municipal council and a mayor elected by the municipal council. According to the 1884 law which, with subsequent amendments, specifies the powers of local government, both the mayor and the municipal council have extensive liberty of action.[2]

Most towns in France are small and, since every town has a mayor, most French mayors are small-town mayors. There is no parallel in France comparable to the American practice of differentiating between incorporated and unincorporated areas. All France is divided into communes: a vast number—nearly 38,000—for a population of forty-six million. With

[1] For the standard history of French communal organization, see Charles Petit-Dutaillis, *Les Communes françaises* (Paris: Albin Michel, 1947).
[2] The legal and financial powers of French local government are summarized in Appendix B.

one-third the population of the other countries in the Common Market, France contains more communes than those of all other member countries combined.[3] Only 3,000 of the 38,000 French communes are considered urban—that is, contain villages with more than 2,000 inhabitants. In the 1950's, only 33.3 per cent of the French lived in cities over 20,000 population, compared to 70.8 per cent of the English.[4] Only one Frenchman in six lives in a city with a population of more than 100,000.[5] (Twice as many Americans, proportionately, live in cities over 100,000.) Indeed, half the communes in France contain fewer than 400 inhabitants.[6] Despite rapid urbanization, one can still traverse large areas of France, pass through hundreds of villages, and not encounter one town whose population exceeds four figures.

French local government provides an opportunity to study French political habits in a particularly direct way. Moreover, the theme of consensus and cleavage, which is central to French politics generally, is particularly relevant to the study of French local politics. French local political habits differ significantly from national practices. Most communes are far less divided by municipal elections than by national elections. A prevailing rhetoric stifles controversy about communal issues. Until now, the issue of consensus at the local level in France has received little scholarly attention. Local political behavior is an important aspect of the French political character that warrants close examination.

Beginning with André Siegfried's *Tableau politique de la France d'ouest sous la troisième république*, electoral sociolo-

[3] Jean-Jacques Delarce, "Réformes territoriales des communes" (unpublished Mémoire, Institut d'Etudes Politiques de Paris, 1962), p. 36.
[4] *United Nations Demographic Yearbook*, 1960 (New York: International Publishers Co., 1961), pp. 264, 367. However, France is urbanizing rapidly. Between the census of 1954 and 1962, the proportion of Frenchmen living in urban centers (over 2,000 inhabitants) rose from 55.9 per cent to 63.0 per cent. *Ibid.*, 1960, p. 386; 1963, p. 210.
[5] *Ibid.*, 1960, p. 364.
[6] *Recensement de 1962: population légale* (Paris: Direction des Journaux Officiels, 1963).

gists have examined temporal changes of local voting patterns in national elections. These studies have provided detailed information on cantonal and even communal voting behavior in national elections.[7] However, studies in electoral sociology are generally concerned with the result of the voting decision rather than with its causes. They do not question *how* local cleavages in national elections develop or are maintained; still less do such studies examine local patterns in *local* elections.

There have been a number of French community studies; these usually examine such issues as voluntary associations, education, and occupational and demographic patterns. Information about local politics can be gleaned from case studies of Auxerre, Grenoble, Magnac, Marigny, Morette, Nouville, Novis, Peyrane-Roussillon, Chanzeaux, and Vienne.[8] However, local politics is not the predominant concern of these studies and, until now, too few communes have been studied to permit meaningful generalizations.[9]

---

[7] For partial bibliographies of French electoral geography, see François Goguel and Alfred Grosser, *La Politique en France* (Paris: Armand Colin, 1964), pp. 101–02; and Alain Lancelot and Jean Ranger, "Développements récents de la recherche électorale en France," *Il Politico*, XXIX (December 1964), 763–87.

[8] Charles Bettelheim and Suzanne Frère, *Une ville française moyenne: Auxerre en 1950* (Paris: Armand Colin, 1951); Christiane Marie, *Grenoble 1871–1965, l'évolution du comportement politique d'une grande ville en expansion* (Paris: Armand Colin, 1966); Julian Pitt-Rivers, "Social-Class in a French Village," *Anthropological Quarterly*, XXXIII (January 1960), 1–13; Roger Josserand, "Rapport d'enquête sur la commune de Marigny en Charolais" (unpublished Mémoire, Institut d'Etudes Politiques de Grenoble, n.d.); J. Garavel, *Les Paysans de Morette, un siècle de vie rurale dans une commune du Dauphiné* (Paris: Armand Colin, 1958); Lucien Bernot and René Blancard, *Nouville, un village français* (Travaux et Mémoires de l'Institut d'Ethnologie, LVII; University of Paris, 1953); Henri Mendras, *Etudes de sociologie rurale: Novis et Virgin* (Paris: Armand Colin, 1951); Laurence Wylie, *Village in the Vaucluse* (New York: Harper & Row, 1964); Wylie (ed.), *Chanzeaux: A Village in Anjou* (Cambridge: Harvard University Press, 1966), and "Social Change at the Grass Roots," in Stanley Hoffmann, *et al.*, *In Search of France* (Cambridge: Harvard University Press, 1963); and Pierre Clément and Nelly Xydias, *Vienne sur le Rhône* (Paris: Armand Colin, 1955).

[9] For example, according to the reports of Pitt-Rivers, *op. cit.*, and Wylie, *Village in the Vaucluse, op. cit.*, local politics in Magnac is quite different

The legal basis of French local government has been thoroughly explored; there are journals that specialize in local government and administrative law, and books that deal with the formal relations between national and local governments.[1] Yet the very term that French writers use to describe the field of local politics—*l'administration locale*—indicates its nonpolitical focus. Scholars usually study local government from the perspective of administrative law; they rarely ask how local officials actually behave. Brian Chapman notes:

Most foreign students of French affairs naturally concentrate on national politics, which is hardly the best introduction to the reality of local administration: on the other hand, many French scholars who concern themselves with political institutions are jurists by training, and are interested in legal concepts rather than political reality.[2]

Specialists also base analyses of French politics upon official election statistics. But the French government publishes individual returns only for the largest cities in France: local election statistics usually represent national totals of elections in all French communes. Global totals are of little assistance in the examination of many issues, and reliance on them may be misleading.

Many years ago, André Siegfried remarked:

It is no wonder that a foreigner is completely at a loss when he tries to understand us, let alone to judge us, for he has no opportunity of meeting the people that we consider most typical of our country.[3]

---

from local politics in Peyrane. Further study would be needed to determine which village was more nearly typical of most French communes.
[1] The leading journals are *La Revue Administrative* and *Départements et communes*; two important books are Charles Schmitt, *Le Maire de la commune rurale* (Paris: Berger-Levrault, 1959); and Brian Chapman, *An Introduction to French Local Government* (London: George Allen & Unwin, 1953).
[2] Chapman, *op. cit.*, p. 219.
[3] André Siegfried, *France: A Study of Nationality* (New Haven: Yale Uni-

French scholars also—either through necessity or choice —seem to be at an equal loss: they have not studied the local politics of their country in great depth. To date, the best general survey of French local government has been written by an Englishman; the best analyses of French communities, by an American![4]

Rather than exploring issues in French administrative law, social structure, and electoral sociology, the present study will investigate a characteristic style of French local politics that has not hitherto been described, a style which will be called local consensus.[5] The aim is to describe the character of local consensus in France, to explore why it exists, and to suggest a critical judgment of its value. Statistical examination of French municipal elections suggests the consensual nature of local politics; interviews with participants provide information about local consensus.

Local consensus is a variable, not a constant: some communes are more united than others and a given commune is more or less united through time. Qualifications are important, yet they should not overshadow the more significant fact of the context in which they occur. It is the basic character of French local consensus that will be emphasized here, rather than its limits.

While the theme of consensus pervades French local politics, it is especially characteristic of small communes, the great majority in France. Although there are similarities between

---

versity Press, 1930), p. 7. Also see Jean Touchard, in the preface to L'As-sociation Française de Science Politique (ed.), *Le Référendum de septem-bre et les élections de novembre 1958* (Paris: Armand Colin, 1960), p. xxii.

[4] Chapman, *op. cit.*, and Wylie, *Village in the Vaucluse, op. cit.* See the reviews of these books in *La Revue française de science politique*, VI (July–September 1956), 672–74; and *ibid.*, VII (October–December 1957), 951–53, respectively. Also see Wylie (ed.), *Chanzeaux, op. cit.*

[5] In order to avoid the cumbersome "local consensus on matters of local concern," the phrase will generally be abbreviated to "local consensus." Unless otherwise stated, the term "local consensus" is not intended to refer to local unity regarding national political issues.

local political patterns in large cities and rural villages, the primary focus of this study is on the small French commune.

French local consensus is based on the strong leadership of the commune's mayor. The mayor's skill in exercising his power discourages opposition to the local government and its policies; the small commune is united under his guidance. Interviews conducted with municipal councilors, mayors, legislators, and government officials provide information about how the mayor exercises his power. The mayor informally organizes the slate of community leaders that is usually victorious in local elections. He virtually monopolizes the initiative of proposing reforms and exercises a veto power over reforms proposed by others. The mayor plays an active role in securing state consent and financial assistance for local projects. His struggles with the national government enhance local unity.

Despite the differences among mayors, most are guided by a particular conception of communal life. They share a rhetoric which opposes political divisions in the commune and which stresses instead the value of communal harmony. The mayor's own efforts to unite the commune help confirm his belief that the commune is naturally united.

The firm and almost entirely unchallenged leadership most mayors exercise hides the fact that local governments are in fact free to make numerous choices and that political principles are relevant to the way in which choices are made. Like the government of any political constituency, French local governments must determine policy. Political choices do exist and the particular choices made by a local government have consequences for the commune. Therefore, in the absence of meaningful alternatives to the decisions of the ruling coalition, how real is the consensus that characterizes most French local governments?

Local governments in France are relatively inactive and do not play a vital role in meeting local needs. Local consensus is more easily obtained because the material and ideological stakes are perceived as low. Furthermore, a widely accepted rhetoric of *apolitisme* asserts that political principles are irrelevant to whatever activity local governments conduct.[6]

The consensus that prevails in most French communes is reminiscent of the harmony characteristic of most French families. The resemblance is heightened by the similar authority patterns in the two units. Much of what has been said about the French family also applies to the French commune. Significantly, a French mayor frequently compares his commune to a family, and characterizes his own role as being that of the commune's father.

One must understand the nature of the French family to appreciate this self-characterization. André Siegfried says, "In France the family is stronger than the state; it provides a social foundation of extraordinary stability."[7]

Far more than in the United States, the life of the French family is rooted in the home. Together, the family and the home form the *foyer*, a word and a concept that are central to understanding French society. Significantly, there is no exact English translation of *foyer*. An American study of French culture does not even try to translate the term.[8]

While the means used for protecting the French home from prying eyes may vary—from a high wall to a concierge— French *foyers* are designed to ensure maximum privacy for their members. What has been said about the architectural means used by the French to secure privacy might be said also about their local political life: "Common to them is the sense of the boundary set, the protection against possible intrusion."[9]

[6] The French term *apolitisme* is retained because there are no satisfactory English equivalents. For a discussion of the doctrine, see Chapter IX.
[7] André Siegfried, "Approaches to an Understanding of Modern France," in Edward M. Earle (ed.), *Modern France* (Princeton, N.J.: Princeton University Press, 1951), p. 11.
[8] Rhoda Métraux and Margaret Mead, *Themes in French Culture* (Stanford, Calif.: Stanford University Press, 1954). Their analysis has proved most helpful for this discussion of French culture.
[9] *Ibid.*, p. 2.

In France, social circles are relatively closed to outsiders; among these circles, the *foyer* is "the most self-contained and enduring."[1] At Peyrane, according to Laurence Wylie, "the family was seen ideally as a strong independent unit: father, mother and children all working together for the common good."[2] The French family is a tightly knit unit and is particularly suspicious of outside intervention. "For the French each family circle is peculiarly self-enclosed, with the family members closely bound to one another and a feeling of extreme wariness about intrusion from the outside."[3]

Consensus within the French family is founded on the father's firm leadership and inequality among family members. A French child "learns to accept an aloof father as the primary source of authority. . . ."[4] Métraux and Mead comment, "In the *foyer*, authority in hands other than those of the father is potentially dangerous to the whole family. . . ."[5]

Compared to their American peers, French children rely less on those outside the family; young children rarely play far from their mothers. One authority observes that the very desire to play with other children is regarded as a weakness in France for it is felt that the family itself should provide sufficient diversion.[6] There are few play facilities in French parks, which increases the child's dependence on his mother.

What one sees in the park, therefore, is not so much groups of children playing together while the adults who have brought them

[1] *Ibid.*, p. 3.
[2] Laurence Wylie, "Social Change at the Grass Roots," in Hoffmann, *et al.*, *op. cit.*, p. 62.
[3] Martha Wolfenstein, "French Parents Take Their Children to the Park," in Margaret Mead and Martha Wolfenstein (eds.), *Childhood in Contemporary Culture* (Chicago: University of Chicago Press, 1955), p. 99.
[4] Jesse Pitts, "Continuity and Change in Bourgeois France," in Hoffmann, *et al.*, *op. cit.*, p. 254.
[5] Métraux and Mead, *op. cit.*, p. 12.
[6] Jesse Pitts, "The Family and Peer Groups," in Norman W. Bell and Ezra F. Vogel (eds.), *A Modern Introduction to the Family* (New York: The Free Press of Glencoe, 1960), p. 267.

for this purpose sit on the sidelines, but rather a series of little family conclaves.[7]

The typical child's reaction to his parents' authority is quite naturally one of respect—and yet also distrust. According to Jesse Pitts, the French child realizes that "in order to protect his individuality he must resort to secrecy and political manipulation."[8]

From the French family experience comes a generalized distrust of outsiders. Françoise Dolto observes that a French child is more distrustful of a psychoanalyst than is an American child.[9] Jesse Pitts relates that the fundamental attitude of the French child is *faut se méfier*—"better be on your guard."[1]

The French attitude toward authority, based on such childhood experiences, affects the conduct of politics. Michel Crozier suggests that, like their children, French adults resent and distrust authority; yet they depend on higher authority to determine the directives that they cannot decide by more democratic procedures. For Crozier, the problem is:

. . . *the disproportion between the authority which seems to us [French] indispensable to govern a human group and the authority that we can accept as members of a group. One might say that we can't bear the authority which, however, we estimate necessary for a united and effective group.*[2]

Crozier suggests that the French dislike either to exercise face-to-face authority or to have such authority exercised over them. Rather than negotiating agreements with one's adver-

---

[7] Wolfenstein, *op. cit.,* p. 100.
[8] Pitts, "Continuity and Change in Bourgeois France," *op. cit.,* p. 254.
[9] Françoise Dolto, "French and American Children as Seen by a French Child Analyst," in Mead and Wolfenstein, *op. cit.,* pp. 409–10.
[1] Pitts, "The Family and Peer Groups," *op. cit.,* p. 281; Pitts, "Continuity and Change in Bourgeois France," *op. cit.,* p. 258.
[2] Michel Crozier, "La France, terre de commandement," *Esprit,* XXV (December 1957), 788. See also Crozier, *The Bureaucratic Phenomenon* (Chicago: University of Chicago Press, 1964), pp. 220–24.

saries, one refers conflicts to a higher authority who will issue unpopular—but, at least, impersonal—directives. In the political sphere this constant recourse to impersonality means that political disputes are not handled at the local level but tend to result in an appeal for state intervention. Stanley Hoffmann points out that the state is called on to exercise centralized but limited authority. The French attempt to have their cake and eat it: to avoid the discomforts of personal responsibility, but without risking a loss of personal privacy and individuality.[3]

Hoffmann describes the pattern of authority that existed in the "republican synthesis" as the "coexistence of limited authoritarianism and potential insurrection against authority."[4] The consequence of permitting a higher authority to arbitrate thus appears to be a loss of individual participation and responsibility. According to Maurice Duverger:

For the French, democracy is first and foremost a system in which the citizen is free, in the sense that he has the possibility to resist the pressure of authority—i.e., the state—to the greatest possible extent. By contrast, in the Anglo-Saxon countries . . . it is thought that democracy is a system which permits the citizen to participate in political decision-making.[5]

While French municipal politics shares elements with French political culture, local politics exhibits distinctive

[3] Hoffmann, *et al.*, *op. cit.*, p. 9. Laurence Wylie observes that the inhabitants of Chanzeaux "willingly delegated the power to run what few affairs they had in common [to their traditional leaders], as long as the leaders in turn exercised their authority with a minimum of interference in the daily life of the individual." (Wylie [ed.], *Chanzeaux, op. cit.*, p. 196.)

[4] *Ibid.*, p. 8. Both Crozier and Hoffmann begin from de Tocqueville's observation, in *The Old Régime and the French Revolution* (Garden City, N.Y.: Anchor Books, 1955), that the French distrust their government, yet turn to it for help at every opportunity.

[5] Maurice Duverger, "The Development of Democracy in France," in Henry W. Ehrmann (ed.), *Democracy in a Changing Society* (New York: Frederick A. Praeger, 1964), p. 69. See also Henry W. Ehrmann, "Direct Democracy in France," *American Political Science Review*, LVII (December 1963), 883–901.

characteristics as well. In most French communes face-to-face
negotiation about local policies is rare: the mayor dominates
the local political life of his commune. He initiates proposals
for local change and guides them to completion. He sponsors
a coalition in local elections that forestalls competition in the
election itself. The mayor's actions thus help ensure that local
conflict will be avoided. On the communal level the mayor
represents the "higher authority" to whom the French have
recourse. The character of French local politics reflects the
mayor's active leadership. Consequently, the manner in which
mayors exercise their powers provides a key to understanding
local consensus in France.

PART I

THE SETTING

Chapter I

A Statistical Examination of Grass-Roots Consensus

The study of French politics has traditionally focused on the central issues of consensus and cleavage. Titles of representative works on French politics are revealing: *In Search of France, France Against Herself, Crisis and Compromise,* and *France Torn.*[1] A foremost scholarly concern has been to explain the high degree of political conflict in France. Numerous explanations have been offered, ranging from France's history to her values, regional diversity, and electoral system.[2] In attempting to learn about French political behavior, however,

[1] Stanley Hoffmann, *et al., In Search of France* (Cambridge: Harvard University Press, 1963); Herbert Luethy, *France Against Herself* (New York: Meridian Books, 1957); Philip M. Williams, *Crisis and Compromise,* 3rd ed. (Hamden, Conn.: Shoe String Press, 1964); and Jacques Fauvet, *La France déchirée* (Paris: Fayard, 1957), which might be translated as *France Torn.* (An English translation is less literal and less revealing: *The Cockpit of France* [London: Harvill, 1960].)

[2] In addition to the works cited in Footnote 1, see Michel Crozier, *The Bureaucratic Phenomenon* (Chicago: University of Chicago Press, 1964), Part Four; Seymour Martin Lipset, *The First New Nation* (New York: Basic Books, 1963), Chaps. 6, 8, 9; and Alexis de Tocqueville, *The Old Régime and the French Revolution* (Garden City, N.Y.: Anchor Books, 1955). For two analyses that minimize the lack of consensus in France, see Nathan Leites, *On the Game of Politics in France* (Stanford, Calif.: Stanford University Press, 1959); and Philip M. Williams, "Political Compromise in France and America," *The American Scholar,* XXVI (Summer 1957), 273–88.

an important source of information has been ignored. French local political patterns contrast sharply with national political patterns; the contrast is relevant to understanding the issues of consensus and cleavage in France.

France is often characterized as a country with high internal conflict.[3] It has frequently been observed that, on the national level, political and social cleavages are deeper and more numerous in France than in the United States. Ideological appeals are said to be more common in France than in America. There is greater class consciousness in France and more hostility among social groups. After a brief period in the Fifth Republic when party conflict declined, political conflict again appears to be high.

What consequences do national cleavages in France have for local politics? One might speculate that political and social divisions in France would have one of two alternative effects on local government. Local politics might simply reflect national political patterns. Since groups are in close proximity on the municipal level, local politics might be at least as ideological and competitive as national politics. Assuming that Frenchmen are involved in local politics, one would expect many political parties to compete for local offices.

Alternatively, Frenchmen might withdraw from local politics altogether. As a result of the relative lack of autonomy of French local government, national political conflicts might dominate popular attention. Because involvement in local government would reinforce existing conflicts, people might simply abstain from participating in local political life.

Thus, two models of French local politics may be posited. Where there is high turnout for local elections, one would also expect there to be high electoral conflict.[4] Great interest in local elections would exacerbate cleavages in the local body

[3] See the works cited in Footnotes 1 and 2 above.
[4] The act of voting is used to measure citizen involvement because turnout can be ascertained and measured relatively easily. Of course, voting alone may demonstrate only minimal political involvement. In *The Civic Culture* (Boston: Little, Brown & Co., 1965), p. 131, Gabriel A. Almond

politic that are influential in national elections. Conversely, low turnout in local elections would lead one to expect a low level of electoral conflict. In the alternative model, the slight interest in local elections, as evidenced by a small proportion of voter turnout, would help keep political tensions low.[5]

Turnout

On the basis of analyses of published national totals, specialists conclude that turnout in France is generally higher in national elections than in local elections. Studying changes in French turnout through time, René Rémond concludes that turnout has been "strongly lower" in local elections than in elections for the National Assembly, "the abstention rate being at least higher and even double."[6]

Jacques Fauvet suggests, "The number of abstentions is nearly always the same, higher in local than in general elections. . . ."[7]

---

and Sidney Verba regard voting "as a relatively passive form of participation in community life, though a form of participation it certainly is."
[5] In *Why Europe Votes* (Chicago: University of Chicago Press, 1930), Harold F. Gosnell found that turnout and competition vary directly in England and France. In England, "the closer the contest the greater is the interest in the election." (*Ibid.*, p. 14.) In France, "the closeness of the contest has a great deal to do with the size of the vote cast. . . ." (*Ibid.*, p. 49.) Studying turnout in France, Jean Meynaud and Alain Lancelot also find that abstentions "tend to diminish when the electoral outcome appears uncertain: the elector becomes more aware of the importance of his participation." (*La Participation des Français à la politique* [Paris: Presses Universitaires de France, 1965], p. 18.) In Swedish local elections, according to Donald R. Niemi, "the presence of competing political lists was related to higher voter participation. . . ." (Niemi, "Sweden's Municipal Consolidation Reforms" [unpublished Ph.D. thesis, University of Chicago, 1966], p. 84.) However, in a review of literature on the question, Robert E. Lane observes that turnout is not necessarily associated with closeness of the election (*Political Life: Why and How People Get Involved in Politics* [Glencoe, Ill.: The Free Press, 1959], pp. 308–10).
[6] René Rémond, "Participation électorale et participation organisée," in Georges Vedel (ed.), *La Dépolitisation: mythe ou réalité?* (Paris: Armand Colin, 1962), p. 78.
[7] Fauvet, *op. cit.*, p. 56.

In a study of turnout in French elections, Jean Meynaud and Alain Lancelot find that "the proportion of abstentions is generally higher for local elections (general council and municipal) [than for legislative elections.]"[8]

According to Nicholas Wahl:

. . . Elections to the municipal councils . . . are influenced mainly by relatively nonpolitical or at least strictly local issues. This, as well as the lack of any real autonomy on the part of these assemblies, makes public interest in local government elections very slight. Nonvoting is, therefore, traditionally widespread. . . .[9]

Jean Stoetzel observes that abstentions in the Fourth Republic were "relatively more frequent in the municipal elections than in the general elections."[1] And François Goguel states unequivocally:

One proof that local political life does not satisfactorily perform the educational role which theorists assign to it is that electoral participation is nearly always weaker in local balloting than in elections to Parliament. Numerous electors are sufficiently interested in national political life to participate in the election of a deputy, but do not bother when it is a question of selecting their commune's municipal council. . . .[2]

Yet two studies of localities that examine turnout in local and national elections find results opposite to those suggested by other scholars. In these areas turnout is higher in local elections than in national elections.[3] In a study of French

[8] Meynaud and Lancelot, *op. cit.*, p. 18.
[9] Nicholas Wahl, "The French Political System," in Samuel H. Beer and Adam B. Ulam (eds.), *Patterns of Government*, 2nd ed. (New York: Random House, 1962), p. 357.
[1] Jean Stoetzel, "Voting Behaviour in France," *The British Journal of Sociology*, VI (June 1955), 105.
[2] François Goguel and Alfred Grosser, *La Politique en France* (Paris: Armand Colin, 1964), p. 58.
[3] Laurence Wylie, *Village in the Vaucluse* (New York: Harper & Row, 1964), p. 233; and Jacques Busnicourt, "Un Canton rural du Santerre," in Jacques Fauvet and Henri Mendras (eds.), *Les Paysans et la politique* (Paris: Armand Colin, 1958), p. 474.

public administration, Ridley and Blondel also observe local turnout and competition patterns to be rather high: "Local elections are keenly contested: a turnout of 75 per cent or 80 per cent is not unusual."[4] According to Alain Lancelot, "Many small communes vote in a massive fashion in local elections; as many people vote as in legislative elections, and even more. In cities, on the contrary, . . . abstentions are nearly always higher [in municipal elections than in legislative elections]."[5] And in 1930 Harold F. Gosnell noted that "popular participation in [French] local elections is not greatly inferior to that in parliamentary elections."[6]

The contradiction can be resolved only by empirical examination. However, there has been no general study until now which has compared the national and local voting patterns in a large number of communes. In the absence of detailed statistics scholars have relied on national electoral totals for information about differences in national and local voting behavior.[7] Because all communes are included together in these totals, significant differences among them may be masked. For example, are comparative turnout rates similar in large and small communes? Reliance on a single national constituency has limited the possibility of more refined analysis and, perhaps more important, has led scholars to reach unjustified conclusions.

A comparison of turnout in national and local elections suggests that, in France as a whole, turnout is higher in national elections. Whereas 75 per cent of all registered French

[4] F. Ridley and J. Blondel, *Public Administration in France* (London: Routledge & Kegan Paul, Ltd., 1964), p. 99.
[5] Alain Lancelot, in the colloquium, "Au Lendemain de l'élection présidentielle," *Revue française de science politique*, XVI (February 1966), p. 178.
[6] Gosnell, *op. cit.*, p. 153.
[7] It is not easy to obtain local election returns in France. Prefectures send only the returns for large cities to the Ministry of the Interior in Paris. For electoral data on all other communes, one must consult the records at each prefecture.

voters cast their ballots in the national elections of November 1958, only 72 per cent of the registered voters went to the polls in municipal elections held four months later.[8] Scholars have generally assumed that turnout patterns in most communes are consistent with the national patterns. Yet this conclusion does not necessarily follow.

From an analysis of turnout based on a large sample of French communes, I have found that, contrary to accepted scholarly opinion, turnout in local elections is extremely high. Moreover, in most communes more Frenchmen vote in local elections than in national elections. Because the reverse is usually true for large communes, the turnout patterns of most French communes have been masked.

In order to study differential turnout, competition, and other factors relating to local consensus, the communes of three French departments were selected for statistical examination. The departments chosen—the Calvados, the Gironde, and the Nord—are in different regions of France and exhibit different economic, social, and political characteristics.[9] There was a total of 1,978 communes in the three departments.[1] For

---

[8] Turnout in the legislative elections of November 23, 1958 is noted in *L'Année politique*, 1958, p. 145. This represents the percentage of valid votes cast (*exprimés*) in relation to registered voters (*inscrits*). For the 1959 municipal elections, the Ministry of the Interior estimated turnout by using all votes cast (*votants*), whether valid or not (*Le Monde*, March 17, 1959). Since the difference between the two measures of turnout is usually about 2 per cent, the Ministry's figure of 73.4 per cent was reduced by about 2 per cent to determine *exprimés*.

[9] Although sampling procedures were not used, an attempt was made to choose departments representative of varying conditions in France. However, as Jean Blondel has noted, "In the case of France, it is very difficult to state whether [a] particular *département* is typical or not: is there anything, from the point of view of social, political or economic life, which can be said to be typical of the whole of France?" ("Local Government and the Ministries in a French *Département*," *Public Administration* [London], XXXVII [Spring 1959], 66.)

[1] Electoral data were obtained from the prefecture in each department. Of the total of 1,978 communes in the three departments, the 95 communes in the *arrondissement* of Vire (Calvados) are excluded because it was impossible to obtain the necessary data. It was also impossible to obtain data for 73 other communes. Thus, 1,810 communes were selected for statistical examination, nearly 5 per cent of all French communes.

each commune, data were collected regarding communal political behavior in local and national elections, the proportion of the municipal council that elected the mayor, and the tenure of the mayor after the 1959 municipal elections.[2]

In the 1958 national elections, average turnout for all communes in the sample—calculating each commune as a unit—was 78.3 per cent. (The national rate for all France—not averaged by commune—was 75 per cent.) In the 1959 local elections, average turnout—again calculating each commune as a unit—was 81.7 per cent. (The comparable figure for all France in the 1959 local elections was 72 per cent.)[3] Thus, on the average, about 3 per cent more Frenchmen in the communes of the sample voted in the local elections of 1959 than in the national elections of 1958. Only 396 of the 1,810 communes studied—less than one-quarter—had lower turnout rates in local elections than in national. In all fourteen *arrondissements* of the three departments, more communes had higher turnout rates for local elections than for national

[2] Figures are from the *premier tour* of each election. The legislative election of November 1958 was chosen since it was nearest in time to the most recent municipal elections—those of March 1959—at the time this study was conducted. Of course, turnout varies in successive elections for the same office. According to unpublished figures made available by the Ministry of the Interior, turnout was lower in the 1959 municipal elections than in any other municipal elections since World War II and lower than in the succeeding municipal elections of 1965. Turnout in the 1958 legislative elections was lower than in previous legislative elections since World War II and lower than in the 1967 legislative elections but was higher than in the succeeding legislative elections of 1962. Moreover, until December 1965, national elections in France meant legislative elections, which are used here for purposes of comparison. Different political patterns prevail for the French presidential elections. For example, turnout was 84.1 per cent in the *premier tour* of the December 1965 presidential elections (*L'Année politique*, 1965, p. 105). Therefore, the hypotheses presented in this statistical examination should be tested against data from other elections.

[3] It is significant that when the percentage of turnout in national elections is averaged by the communes in the sample or totaled for all France and the percentage taken, the two methods of calculating turnout produce similar results. The same is not true for turnout in local elections. This suggests that size of commune affects turnout in local elections more than in national elections, an hypothesis that will be supported by evidence presented below.

elections. Indeed, except for the *arrondissements* of Dunkerque and Lille, more than two-thirds of the communes in each *arrondissement* had higher turnout rates in local than in national elections.

A large proportion of Frenchmen in the communes of the sample turned out to elect a deputy in 1958. However, in most communes even more Frenchmen went to the polls several months later to elect a municipal council. Contrary to generally accepted findings, turnout in French communes is frequently higher in local than in legislative elections.

The higher rate of turnout in local elections is also evident when departmental voting patterns are analyzed. Differences in turnout between national and local elections were compared for France's eighty-nine metropolitan departments.[4] In more than two-thirds of all departments (64 out of 89) turnout was greater in the municipal elections of 1959 than in the national elections of 1958.[5]

[4] Unpublished election returns were made available by the Bureau of Elections, Ministry of the Interior. Aggregate returns (those compiled by adding together all returns from all communes) were used for comparison rather than average-based figures (figures obtained by averaging the turnout percentages for all communes taken one by one). Judging from the table in Footnote 5, turnout in local elections would be higher if the calculation was based on average-based figures.
[5] The proportion was reversed for turnout based on aggregate totals in the three departments chosen for close study. In two, turnout was higher in national elections than in local. This suggests that the finding regarding higher turnout in local elections holds elsewhere in France, where even aggregate-based turnout percentages are higher in local than in national elections.

Differential Per Cent Turnout, by Department

DEPARTMENT	AGGREGATE-BASED		AVERAGE-BASED	
	National (1958)	Local (1959)	National (1958)	Local (1959)
Calvados	75.4%	78.1%	76.4%	82.2%
Gironde	74.2	71.8	74.0	81.1
Nord	82.6	80.9	84.5	85.7

Average turnout was calculated for each of the cantons in the three departments of the sample by averaging turnout rates in the communes comprising the canton. In more than three-fourths of all cantons—113 of 146—average turnout was higher in the 1959 municipal elections than in the 1958 national elections.

In order to study further the relation between turnout and size of commune, communes were stratified by size into four groups, and turnout in local and national elections was compared for each group.

Table 1
Differential Turnout in Communes of Different Size

| AVERAGE POPULATION, 1959 | NUMBER OF COMMUNES | PER CENT TURNOUT | |
		National (1958)	Local (1959)
Below 400	799	76.9%	83.0%
401–700	325	77.2	82.5
701–2,000	416	80.4	82.0
Over 2,000	270	80.4	76.5

Table 1 reveals an important relation between size of commune and turnout. The relation is opposite in national elections compared to local elections: in national elections, turnout varies directly with size of commune; in local elections, on the other hand, turnout varies inversely with size of commune. As the size of commune increases, turnout tends to increase in national elections and decrease in local elections.[6]

[6] Turnout also appears to be affected by a regional factor independent of the size of commune. Communes in the department of the Nord have a far higher average turnout rate in both local and national elections than communes in either of the other two departments. See the table in Footnote 5 on page 24.

French turnout patterns in national and local elections appear opposite to Norwegian turnout patterns. Norwegian cities and rural communes

The installation of modern tabulating equipment enabled the Ministry of the Interior to publish more detailed returns for the municipal elections of March 14, 1965 than for previous elections. These figures permit a replication of the comparison between turnout in large and small communes.

As suggested by some reports, interest in the 1965 local elections—as measured by voting turnout—was higher than in previous local elections.[7] Turnout for all France in 1965 was 75 per cent, compared to the turnout figure of 72 per cent in the 1959 municipal elections.[8] A comparison of turnout figures for large and small communes in the 1965 municipal elections corroborates the earlier finding. The Ministry of the Interior divided communes into those with populations greater and less than 30,000, in accordance with the different electoral laws used in 1965 for the two categories of communes. There was a very great difference in turnout between large cities and other communes. Whereas turnout was 67.5 per cent in large communes, it was 78.5 per cent in all other communes.[9]

Thus, analysis of French voting behavior reveals that municipal elections attract surprisingly high turnout. Contrary to general scholarly opinion, in most communes turnout is higher for local elections than for national elections.

---

both have higher turnout patterns in national than local elections; moreover, the discrepancy between turnout in national and local elections is higher for rural communes than for cities. See Stein Rokkan and Henry Valen, "The Mobilization of the Periphery: Data on Turnout, Party Membership and Candidate Recruitment in Norway," in "Approaches to the Study of Political Participation," *Acta Sociologica*, VI, no. 1–2 (1962), 118 and 142; and Ulf Torgersen, "The Trend Towards Political Consensus: The Case of Norway," *ibid.*, p. 166.

[7] Edmond Taylor, "French Politics at the Municipal Level," *The Reporter* (April 8, 1965), p. 32; and François Goguel, "Les Elections municipales des 14 et 21 mars 1965: la signification de la consultation," *Revue française de science politique*, XV (October 1965), 912.

[8] *L'Année politique*, 1965, p. 20.

[9] In the 1959 municipal elections, aggregate turnout for the eight communes of the sample that were over 30,000 was 70.9 per cent, as compared with 80.2 per cent aggregate turnout for all communes in the sample under 30,000.

Competition

Since there is high turnout in French local elections, in accordance with the previous discussion one would expect local politics to be characterized by high conflict. High turnout in local elections presumably reflects the presence of extensive competition for municipal office. Given the generally high competition that prevails in French national elections, cleavages in a given commune's local voting behavior appear to parallel cleavages in the commune's national voting behavior.

In order to test the hypothesis that turnout follows competition, electoral competition for the communes of the sample was measured and compared. An "index of multipartyism" was used to measure competition in national and local elections.[1] The index measures the degree to which votes in a commune are distributed among competing candidates or lists. It increases as the number of candidates or lists competing increases and as the proportions of the total vote received by candidates or lists converge. The value of the index lies in its ability to measure the closeness of the electoral outcome in multiparty systems.[2]

[1] The formula for the "index of multipartyism" was suggested by Duncan MacRae, Jr. It is:

$$I = \text{antilog}_e \left\{ - \sum_{i}^{k} p_i \log_e p_i \right\}$$

where: k = number of candidates or lists; p_i = proportion of vote for ith list; $\Sigma_i p_i = 1$. Lists or candidates receiving less than 5 per cent of the vote were eliminated from calculation of the index. The index has also been used in the social sciences by Glaucio Ary Dillon Soares and Amelia Maria Carvalho de Noronha, "Urbanização e Dispersão Eleitorae," *Revista de Direito Público e Ciencia Politica*, III (July–December 1960), 258–70.

[2] The index does not exactly measure conflict or competition but rather the convergence of votes among competing parties. Competition and conflict are dependent on electoral laws and other factors, in addition to the distribution of votes among candidates. However, since the closeness of the election is a critical aspect of competition, the terms "competition" and "conflict" will be used below to refer to the index of multipartyism.

For each commune in the sample, an index of multi-partyism was constructed to measure the commune's voting behavior in the 1958 legislative election and in the 1959 municipal election. Voting patterns in the tiny commune of Campigny (Calvados) illustrate the index of multipartyism. In the local elections of 1959, 75 of Campigny's 94 registered voters went to the polls. The commune split its vote between two lists, one of which received an average of 46 votes, the other an average of 13 votes.[3] Isolated candidates received an average of 3 votes.[4] Campigny's index of multipartyism in the 1959 local elections was 1.70.

In the national elections of 1958, Campigny split its vote more evenly and among a larger number of candidates. Seventy of the 96 voters registered in 1958 cast valid ballots in the legislative elections that year. Two candidates for deputy each received 30 votes, a third candidate received 6 votes, and the fourth candidate received the remaining 4 votes. Campigny's index of multipartyism for this election was therefore 3.01.

The voters of Campigny were thus more divided about their choice of a deputy to the National Assembly than they were about the selection of their municipal council. The commune distributed its votes more widely in national elections than in local elections. Moreover, the proportions of votes cast for candidates for deputy were more similar to each other than were the proportions of votes for competing lists in local elections. Campigny's voting behavior does not conform to the predicted pattern.

[3] The total of the averages for the lists does not equal the total number voting. For the municipal elections of March 1959, voters in small communes were not required to vote for an entire list and could delete or substitute names if they wished. Therefore, different candidates on a list might not receive the same number of votes. For the calculations here, the number of votes on a given list was determined by averaging the votes received by the candidate with most votes on the list and those of the candidate with fewest votes on the list.

[4] Since the average of 3 votes was less than 5 per cent of the total cast, the 3 votes were eliminated from calculation of the index.

Yet, contrary to expectation, Campigny's voting patterns resembled those in most French communes. Judging from the communes of the sample, competition for local office is generally low in France. A comparison of competition in national and local elections reveals that competition is much less widespread in local elections than it is in national. In virtually every commune there is far greater fractionalization of the vote for national elections than for local elections.

The mean index of multipartyism for the 1958 national election for all communes in the sample is 3.37, as compared with a mean index of 1.64 for the 1959 local elections. In only 2 of the 146 cantons in the sample was average competition higher in local than in national elections. Competition was greater for local than national elections in a mere 85 of the 1,810 communes studied. Rather than competition being greater in local elections, as the figures on turnout might suggest, it is significantly lower than in national elections.

Despite the greater competition in French national elections compared to local elections, turnout is generally higher for local elections. It would seem, therefore, that local elections attract greater interest than national elections. Yet, for any given election, one would still expect there to be a direct relation between competition and turnout. In order to test the hypothesis that, for any given election, turnout and competition vary directly, the 1959 local elections were selected. The turnout rate in the fifty communes of the sample with the highest competition was compared with the turnout rate in

Table 2
Relations Between Competition and Turnout,
Local Elections (1959)

LEVEL	INDEX OF COMPETITION	PER CENT TURNOUT
High	3.45	79.7%
Low	1.00	80.2

the fifty communes with lowest competition. The results are shown in Table 2.

Table 2 shows an inverse relation between competition and turnout in local elections. This surprising finding was corroborated by multiple regression analysis, which showed turnout to be fairly significant in explaining competition. Once again, there was a negative correlation between turnout and competition in local elections: as turnout decreases, competition increases. The expected relation between turnout and competition is not confirmed by these data.[5]

Since turnout also decreases as size of commune increases, does size of commune have any effect on the extent of competition in French elections? Size of commune proves to have a different effect on the extent of competition in national as compared to local elections. In the sample as a whole, competition in local elections was rather highly associated with the size of commune: +.35. Thus, as size of commune increases, there is a tendency toward greater competition in local elections.[6] By contrast, the correlation of the size of commune with degree of competition in national elections is a mere +.03. In national elections, the degree of cleavages within a commune does not appear to be significantly influenced by

[5] The relation between turnout and competition in the 1958 national election was less clear. Turnout and competition were inversely related for the fifty communes in the sample with highest competition and the fifty communes with lowest competition. However, multiple regression analysis showed the turnout rate to be relatively unimportant in explaining competition in the 1958 national elections.

[6] Responses to a French public opinion poll furnish additional evidence that national and local cleavages are quite distinct and that they more nearly coincide as the size of commune increases. French voters were asked: "In choosing among candidates in municipal elections, are you concerned to know their attitudes toward General de Gaulle's policy?" Far more of those questioned replied "No" than "Yes." In rural communes, three-fourths of the respondents were not concerned about local candidates' attitudes toward de Gaulle's policies. The proportion of respondents who were concerned was higher in big cities: Jeanne Piret, "L'Opinion publique au début de l'année 1965," *Revue française de science politique*, XV (June 1965), 536.

the commune's size: national elections tend to divide small communes only slightly less than they divide large communes. In local elections, size of commune plays a far more important role: cleavages in local elections appear to become much less sharp as the size of commune diminishes. Small towns are far less divided by local elections than are large cities.

The effect of size can be seen more clearly in Table 3, where competition in the fifty largest communes in the sample is compared with competition in the fifty smallest communes.

Table 3
Differential Competition in Large and Small Communes

	COMPETITION	
REGISTERED VOTERS	National (1958)	Local (1959)
High 32,511	3.79	3.07
Low 70	2.61	1.55

When we compare communes of different size, we find less spread between competition in national elections than competition in local elections. In national elections, the index of multipartyism for small communes is more than two-thirds of that for large communes. Regarding the choice of a deputy to the National Assembly, small towns are nearly as divided as large cities. In local elections, on the other hand, the index of multipartyism for small communes is one-half of that for large cities. Regarding the choice of local governmental leaders, small towns are far more united than large cities.

The proportion of municipal councilors elected on the first ballot is another measure of community conflict, since a candidate must receive an absolute majority of the popular vote to be elected on the first ballot. Once again, conflict in local elections appears to be lower in small communes than in large. In the fifty largest communes, an average of 25.3 per cent of

the municipal council was elected on the first ballot.[7] Far
greater agreement prevailed in the fifty smallest communes,
where an average of 87.8 per cent of the municipal council
was elected on the first ballot.

Regardless of size, then, French communes are quite
divided by national elections, although small communes are
somewhat less divided than large communes. Moreover, in
most French communes, competition is higher in national
than in local elections. In large communes, competition is
fairly high for local office and cleavages in national elections
are only moderately higher than in local elections. In small
communes there is a greater disparity in competition: while
national elections divide small communes nearly as much as
they divide large communes, local elections divide small communes far less than large communes. Thus, national and local
cleavages more nearly coincide in large communes than in
small communes.

There is little direct relation, however, between cleavages
in French national and local elections. This lack of relation
becomes apparent when one compares the fifty communes in
the sample where competition was highest in the 1959 local
elections, with the fifty communes where competition was
lowest (Table 4). Although competition in local elections was

Table 4

National Cleavages in Communes of
High and Low Cleavage, Municipal Elections (1959)

	COMPETITION	
	Local (1959)	National (1958)
High	3.46	3.75
Low	1.00	3.31

[7] The communes of Bordeaux and Lille, which were larger than 120,000
and consequently elected their municipal councils by proportional representation, are excluded from this calculation.

much higher in one group of communes than in the other, competition in national elections in one group was practically the same as in the other.

An even more striking result occurs when two groups of communes are isolated according to high and low competition in the 1958 national elections. Comparing these two groups (Table 5), there is a slightly *inverse* relation between competition in national and local elections.[8]

Table 5
Local Cleavages in Communes of High and Low Cleavage, National Elections (1958)

	COMPETITION	
National (1958)		*Local* (1959)
High 5.53		1.60
Low 1.53		1.81

The foregoing statistical analysis partially corroborates the dissensual nature of French national politics described by other observers using different methods. Furthermore, unlike the United States, cleavages in French national elections are nearly as great in small towns as in large cities.[9] However, statistical analysis reveals a marked contrast between political

[8] While size of commune helps explain competition in local elections, it does not nullify the previous finding that turnout is negatively related to competition. In a multiple regression analysis, both turnout and size of commune independently affect local electoral competition and, in fact, turnout plays a far more important role than size of commune.

[9] Cf. Angus Campbell, Philip E. Converse, Warren E. Miller, and Donald E. Stokes, *The American Voter* (New York: John Wiley & Sons, 1960), Chaps. 13 and 15; V. O. Key, *Public Opinion and American Democracy* (New York: Alfred A. Knopf, 1964), pp. 110–18; and Duncan MacRae, Jr., "Occupations and the Congressional Vote," *American Sociological Review*, XX (Spring 1955), 332–40; "Religious and Socioeconomic Factors in French Voting, 1946–56," *American Journal of Sociology*, LXIV (November 1958), 290–98; and *Parliament, Parties, and Society in France, 1946–1958* (New York: St. Martin's Press, 1967), Chap. 8.

patterns in local and national elections that has not been adequately noted in the scholarly literature on French politics: local elections almost invariably produce less conflict than national elections. This is particularly true of small communes, but it was also found to be characteristic of some of the largest cities in France.

Tenure of Mayor

Figures on mayoral tenure further demonstrate the extent of communal consensus on local issues. Low turnover in local office is a corollary of low competition for local office. Since a French mayor is elected by his commune's municipal council, figures on mayoral stability in office probably indicate relative contentment within the municipal council and the commune.

The mayors of most communes in the sample held office for long periods. The average tenure was calculated for all mayors in the sample after the 1959 municipal elections. Thus, mayors were included who were elected for the first time in 1959 as well as incumbents re-elected to another term in office. The average tenure of the mayors in the sample was 9.6 years. Put another way, a typical mayor elected in 1959 had already been elected either once or twice before.[1] And the typical mayor could now confidently look forward to adding *another* six years to his previous nine years of service as mayor before the next municipal elections.[2]

Moreover, a man was not likely to be elected mayor without having first served an apprenticeship as municipal councilor. The mayors in the sample were municipal councilors an average of 6.4 years (more than one term) before they were elected chief executives of their communes.

[1] The French mayor is elected for a six-year term.
[2] There was also great stability in the municipal elections of March 1965. See Goguel, "Les Elections municipales des 14 et 21 mars 1965," *loc. cit.*, and Philip M. Williams, "Party, Presidency and Parish Pump in France," *Parliamentary Affairs*, XVIII (Summer 1965), 257–65.

There was some variation in mayoral tenure according to size of commune. Mayors from both the largest and smallest communes in the sample generally held office longer than other mayors in the sample. The average terms of mayors from the fifty largest communes was 12.2 years. Mayors of tiny communes were especially secure: those from the fifty smallest communes had held office for an average of 20.8 years!

One might have expected the change in regime from the Fourth to the Fifth Republic to affect patterns of local office-holding. Yet mayoral turnover was low, despite the important changes occurring in national politics and the fundamental change in the political system itself.

It is instructive in this regard to compare the turnover rates of mayors and deputies. In the 1956 legislative elections, the last legislative elections held in the Fourth Republic, 62 per cent of the incumbent deputies—336 out of 544 deputies—were re-elected to the National Assembly.[3] The proportion of incumbent deputies who were re-elected dropped sharply in the first elections held after the advent of the Fifth Republic. In the legislative elections of 1958 most incumbents were beaten: only 23 per cent—131 out of 537 deputies—secured re-election.[4]

Municipal elections took place less than four months later, and, since the previous municipal elections had been held well before the end of the Fourth Republic, one might have expected the rate of turnover to be as high among mayors as

[3] Mattei Dogan, "Les Candidats et les élus," in Maurice Duverger, François Goguel, and Jean Touchard (eds.), Les Elections du 2 janvier 1956 (Paris: Armand Colin, 1957), p. 446; and Dogan, "Political Ascent in a Class Society: French Deputies, 1870–1958," in Dwaine Marvick (ed.), Political Decision-makers (New York: The Free Press of Glencoe, 1961), pp. 57–90.

[4] L'Année politique, 1958, p. 146. One reason was that the size of the National Assembly was reduced. For a study examining the defeat of Fourth Republic politicians in Fifth Republic elections, see Mattei Dogan, "Le Personnel politique et la personnalité charismatique," Revue française de sociologie, VI (July–September 1965), 305–24.

among deputies. In fact, however, there was extraordinary stability among local officeholders. Turnover among mayors between the local elections of 1953 and 1959 was markedly lower than it was among deputies between the legislative elections of 1956 and 1958. Even more striking, a significantly larger proportion of mayors remained in office between 1953 and 1959 than did deputies between the two Fourth Republic elections of 1951 and 1956. Only one-fourth of all mayors—444 out of 1,810—were elected for the first time in 1959. Most mayors were initially elected during the Fourth Republic and were re-elected in 1959.[5] Thus, the great stability of tenure among French mayors becomes particularly noteworthy when contrasted with the much shorter tenure of French deputies.[6]

Conclusion

In light of national political patterns, a statistical examination of local politics in France raises almost as many questions as it answers. French local governments have been dismissed as unimportant because of their relative lack of autonomy. Yet citizen interest—as measured by voting turnout —is high. The high turnout rate for local elections in most French communes is particularly striking juxtaposed with the relative lack of conflict in these elections.[7]

[5] Moreover, the higher attrition rate occurred in a shorter time period. Whereas the previous elections for mayor had taken place six years earlier, those for deputy occurred only two years before.

[6] "Many Gaullists who swept to the Assembly in a wave of protest in 1958 were surprised to see the 'man of the System' they had expelled from Parliament comfortably returned to his mayoral chair six months later." (Philip M. Williams, Crisis and Compromise, 3rd ed. [Hamden, Conn.: Shoe String Press, 1964], pp. 331–32.)

[7] Our findings corroborate what Georges Lavau has noted: citizens "may not vote in the same manner in local elections, national elections, referendums, etc." (Lavau, "Les Aspects socio-culturels de la dépolitisation," in Vedel [ed.], op. cit., p. 197.) François Goguel and André Philip have also noted that French local elections differ from national elections.

Political scientists generally assume that turnout varies in response to the closeness of an election. Yet study of French local elections suggests there is no necessary link between electoral turnout and competition. Given the low competition in local elections, why is turnout high? Why, in fact, is particularly low competition in local elections associated with particularly high turnout? Moreover, while the size of the political unit helps to explain the turnout rate, size does not influence turnout in a constant fashion. In French national elections, turnout increases as the size of commune increases. Why is the pattern reversed in local elections, where turnout diminishes as the size of commune increases?

French communes appear to exhibit a degree of consensus on local matters that does not prevail with regard to national political issues. In most French communes, especially small ones, there is significantly less competition in local elections than in national. French mayors remain in office far longer than French deputies. How does the typical mayor achieve local unity in face of the sharp cleavages dividing his commune in national elections?

(Goguel, *loc. cit.*, p. 917; Philip, in Léo Hamon [ed.], *Les Nouveaux comportements de la classe ouvrière* [Paris: Presses Universitaires de France, 1962], p. 128.)

Portrait of a Mayor

🌸 *"La plus belle chose du monde, c'est d'être maire de son pays."*[1] While few respondents were as candid as this mayor, who presided over a commune in Alsace, every mayor interviewed appeared to derive great pride from his municipal mandate. The French mayor's prestige helps him to maintain communal solidarity on local issues. A French mayor regards himself—and is regarded—as an extremely important personage. An article about a French mayor begins, "The municipal employee looked at the mayor as if at an icon."[2]

The prestige that the mayor enjoys may surprise foreign observers. Brian Chapman notes that, despite the fact that local governments in England are more autonomous than in France, "the French mayor has considerably greater personal prestige and personal power than his English counterpart."[3] In the United States, too, with a federal system and a strong

---

[1] "The most beautiful thing in the world is to be mayor of one's locality." Quoted in François-André Plaisant, "L'Avenir de la petite commune dans le Haut-Rhin" (unpublished Mémoire, Ecole Nationale d'Administration, Paris, 1958), p. 26.

[2] Michel Vianey, "A quoi sert un maire?" *L'Express*, April 18, 1963, p. 19.

[3] Brian Chapman, *An Introduction to French Local Government* (London: George Allen & Unwin, 1953), p. 19.

tradition of local autonomy, it is doubtful whether comparably high status is attached to the position of mayor.

According to a study of eighteenth-century municipal administration in Brittany, the mayor was "always among the most distinguished men in the city that he administered."[4] The importance of the office has not altered fundamentally since. Prior to World War II, an observer of French local government wrote that the French mayor "has acquired a prestige little short of remarkable. . . ."[5] More recently, a French public opinion poll revealed that when rural residents were asked to name the most important local resident in their area the mayor ranked with the largest landowner.[6]

In France the choice of mayor is extremely important. What qualities are sought in a mayor? Lucien Bernot and René Blancard report that the voters of Nouville seek *un monsieur*—a person of substance.[7] Laurence Wylie specifies that a mayor must be *sérieux*. The men elected to municipal office at Peyrane are supposed to "mind their own business and seem indifferent to the affairs of other people."[8]

---

[4] Antoine Dupuy, *Etudes sur l'administration municipale en Bretagne au XVIIIe siècle* (Paris: Picard, 1891), p. 41.
[5] Walter Rice Sharp, "Local Government in France," in William Anderson (ed.), *Local Government in Europe* (New York: Appleton-Century-Crofts, 1939), p. 147. According to Laurence Wylie, the municipal council of Chanzeaux, under the mayor's leadership, "receives the highest degree of respect accorded any group by the commune's population." (Wylie [ed.], *Chanzeaux: A Village in Anjou* [Cambridge: Harvard University Press, 1966], p. 227.)
[6] Quoted in Roger Aubin, *Communes et démocratie, I: taches et moyens de la commune* (Paris: Les Editions Ouvrières, 1965), p. 14. Cf. the position of the southern Italian mayor described by Edward Banfield, in *The Moral Basis of a Backward Society* (Glencoe, Ill.: The Free Press, 1958), p. 27.
[7] Lucien Bernot and René Blancard, *Nouville, un village français* (Travaux et Mémoires de l'Institut d'Ethnologie, LVII; University of Paris, 1953), p. 241.
[8] Laurence Wylie, *Village in the Vaucluse* (New York: Harper & Row, 1964), p. 6. One might speculate that the reason is precisely that these men acquire power to intervene in men's affairs. See also Wylie (ed.), *Chanzeaux, op. cit.*, pp. 196, 207, and 227–32.

One mayor described the qualities desirable in a mayor:

The mayor is a prominent man. He must possess un petit bagage *(a stock-in-trade). He must be perfectly honest, have good sense, and serve as an example to his constituents. He must be progressive; he can't stand still.*[9]

While the office of mayor is a political office, the qualities that are needed to be a mayor extend beyond the espousal of partisan principles. A study of mayors in a canton near Paris finds that, for local office, "One doesn't vote for *un homme de politique* but for *un brave homme.*"[1] In another canton, the authority mayors have "does not depend on their political opinions but rather on the fact that they were elected by nearly unanimous vote of their councilors. . . ."[2] At Grenoble, "Voters prefer responsible men rather than militant politicians to administer their city. Local leaders are successful because of their social position and administrative capacities, not because of their political opinions, which differ from those held by most inhabitants of Grenoble."[3]

The mayor is expected to be more than the leader of the winning political party. An observer of French local government suggests that "the mayor naturally becomes the guide of his constituents, not only in their relations with the government but also in regard to their private affairs."[4] The French word *notable* suggests the fusion of high social status and political position and, as one study notes, "Merely because

[9] From an interview conducted with a mayor in the Gironde, February 6, 1963. Since respondents were promised anonymity, quotations from interviews will hereafter be given without further citation.
[1] Hélie de Noailles, "Le Maire face aux problèmes communaux dans la région parisienne" (unpublished Mémoire, Institut d'Etudes Politiques de Paris, 1964), p. 17.
[2] Eric Degremont, "Les Maires ruraux, leur autorité" (unpublished Mémoire, Institut d'Etudes Politiques de Paris, 1965), p. 42.
[3] Christiane Marie, *Grenoble 1871–1965, l'évolution du comportement politique d'une grande ville en expansion* (Paris: Armand Colin, 1966), pp. 37–38.
[4] Charles Schmitt, *Le Maire de la commune rurale* (Paris: Berger-Levrault, 1959), p. 30.

of his elected position, the municipal magistrate becomes a veritable *notable*."[5] A study of rural mayors suggests a complementary process: "Rather than the position of mayor actually conferring authority, it gives formal support to the informal authority a local *notable* already has because of his character and social position."[6]

The choice of mayor frequently appears to be nearly self-evident. At Nouville, "even the mayor's greatest critics recognize that he is indispensable."[7] When asked about his chances for re-election, a mayor replied simply, "Once elected, a mayor remains in office for life."[8]

Lucien Gachon describes the reasoning of voters deliberating on the choice of local governors: "Who can better govern the commune, the canton, or the *arrondissement*, than the man who can govern himself successfully and well?"[9] Mayors are usually among the wealthy—and conservative—men of their commune. Conservative mayors are especially apt to be found in small communes, as Table 6 indicates.

Large communes are far more likely than small communes to elect a Communist, non-Communist left, or Socialist mayor. Although only one-fifth of all mayors of the Calvados, Gironde, and Nord are of the left, there are proportionately more than twice as many leftist mayors in communes over 2,000. Patterns in the largest French cities appear virtually identical to

[5] Jean Claude le Taillandier de Gabory, "Les Conseillers généraux en Gironde depuis 1919" (unpublished Mémoire, Institut d'Etudes Politiques de Bordeaux, 1959), p. 22.

[6] Degremont, *op. cit.*, p. 33.

[7] Bernot and Blancard, *op. cit.*, p. 25. See also Wylie (ed.), *Chanzeaux, op. cit.*, pp. 228–32.

[8] From unpublished interview notes which Thierry de Beaucé generously made available. Other quotations from his notes will be cited hereafter as "De Beaucé interviews." See also de Beaucé's study, "Opinions et attitudes des maires ruraux" (unpublished Mémoire, Institut d'Etudes Politiques de Paris, 1964).

[9] Lucien Gachon, "L'Arrondissement d'Ambert," in Jacques Fauvet and Henri Mendras (eds.), *Les Paysans et la politique* (Paris: Armand Colin, 1958), p. 408.

Table 6

Party of Mayor in Communes of Different Size

(in per cent)

PARTY	POPULATION				
	0–399	400–699	700–1999	2000 and over	Total
Communist	0.3%	1.9%	5.2%	14.9%	3.8%
Non-Communist left	1.4	1.6	2.2	1.2	1.6
Socialist	6.9	13.4	18.5	29.1	14.0
Radical	12.1	17.2	17.7	8.4	13.6
MRP	5.3	4.4	9.1	11.9	7.0
UNR	16.9	9.0	10.6	13.4	13.5
Independent	56.0	51.6	36.8	21.0	45.6
Far right	1.4	0.9	–	–	0.8

SOURCE: Based on unpublished figures made available by the Ministry of the Interior, 1964.

patterns in communes of the sample over 2,000. Prior to the 1965 municipal elections, 45 per cent of the mayors in all French cities over 30,000 were Communist, non-Communist left, or Socialist.[1] Marcel Jollivet has observed that even a village voting "left" in national elections frequently elects a conservative mayor.[2] "The peasant world hasn't stopped voting for the *notable* in local elections."[3]

Gordon Wright describes a commune which votes very differently in national and local elections. The village of Epagny, near Soissons, consistently voted Communist after World War II, the Communist vote in the commune varying

[1] *Le Monde*, March 13, 1965.
[2] However, a global comparison of political party totals between national and local elections is difficult. Since lists in most communes contain members from rival national political parties, one cannot total the vote by party in municipal elections. A comparison between party distributions of municipal councilors and deputies is given in Table 7, Chapter VII.
[3] Marcel Jollivet, "Le Canton d'Orgères-en-Beauce," in Fauvet and Mendras (eds.), *op. cit.*, p. 461.

between 45–61 per cent in national elections. However, during the same period not one Communist had been elected to the municipal council—and the Conservative son of the former (Conservative) mayor was repeatedly re-elected mayor. In reply to questions about this curious contradiction, a typical explanation for supporting the mayor went: "He's not like most of the big shots; he's a *chic* type. And besides, who else around here could be mayor?"[4]

Although French mayors are alike in certain respects, an onlooker at a meeting of mayors is struck by the enormous diversity of those present. Sitting side by side with simple men who lead rural communes of a few score inhabitants are nationally prominent deputies and cabinet ministers. One way to distinguish mayors is by the metaphors they use to describe themselves and their relationship to the commune. The self-description small-town mayors most commonly gave was, in the words of one, that "the mayor is like the father of a communal family." In a collection of model speeches for mayors, it is suggested that the mayor say about himself and his municipal council, "We attempt to administer the interests entrusted to us as fathers of the family."[5] The mayor who saw himself as father of the commune proudly told about the demanding nature of his position. One mayor summarized his role: "My constituents regard me as a priest. They visit my home if they need advice. They tell me about everything that concerns the commune." His town clerk added proudly, "It's not like that at Langoiran or Cadillac [two nearby communes]."

After stopping to chat with an elderly woman in his commune, another mayor related an example of his informal

[4] Quoted in Gordon Wright, *Rural Revolution in France* (Stanford, Calif.: Stanford University Press, 1964), pp. 188–89. See also Wright, "Four Red Villages in France," *Yale Review*, L (March 1952), 361–72, which contains further information about the village.

[5] Pierre-Paul Armand, *Guide pratique de l'orateur municipal* (Paris: Publications Administratives, 1959), p. 10.

duties. Although the commune granted the aged constituent social assistance, the amount was insufficient. The mayor said that he had tried to persuade the woman's son to contribute toward her support; in addition, the mayor personally supplemented her income out of his own pocket.

In some areas, it is common practice for mayors to divide a deceased constituent's possessions among his offspring at their request, thus helping the family avoid the disgrace of a legal dispute.[6]

Most efforts of mayors calling themselves communal fathers were directed toward maintaining harmony and happiness within the commune, rather than sponsoring innovations in communal life. A mayor was more involved with granting personal favors to constituents than with handling matters of more widespread communal concern. The commune he administered was small, traditional, and rural. His commune was losing population as younger residents left for more promising positions elsewhere. Due to emigration, small towns in France are becoming even smaller.

The mayors who called themselves communal fathers were traditional *notables*, whose authority was informal and diffuse. Most were elderly men. (According to Charles d'Aragon, "The only place where a man of 45 can harbor the illusion of being young is at a meeting of mayors of his department."[7]) They had held office since World War II; some had been mayor even before the war. Most of them had ties in the commune going back generations; and their forebears were also likely to have been elected to local office: on a tour of one town hall the mayor proudly pointed to a plaque that commemorated his grandfather's thirty years of service as mayor of the commune.

Mayors who characterized themselves as communal fathers

---

[6] Charles Schmitt, *Le Maire de la commune rurale* (Paris: Berger-Levrault, 1959), pp. 30–31.
[7] Charles d'Aragon, "Le Village et les pouvoirs," in Fauvet and Mendras (eds.), *op. cit.*, p. 509. Wylie (ed.), *Chanzeaux, op. cit.*, p. 229, also stresses the fact that, traditionally, local leaders were elderly men.

were highly devoted to their elected position and to their commune. They were often at the town hall and always willing to entertain requests for help.[8] In fact, a constituent would not hesitate to come to the mayor's house with a problem, if the mayor were not to be found at the town hall. Several mayors grumbled, during interviews, about these "intrusions," but it was quite evident that they regarded the visits as confirmation of their own importance.

Mayors who saw themselves as fathers of the commune devoted several hours a day to the informal tasks connected with their mandate. Some were retired; most of the others worked in the commune of which they were mayor, and their profession allowed them much free time. For example, one mayor owned a small textile factory, managed by his brother; another owned a pharmacy, managed by his wife. Both mayors were thus able to devote themselves to communal affairs.

Unlike Americans, Frenchmen are unable to agree on a political hero whom they could designate as the "father of his country."[9] Nonetheless, in thousands of small French communes the mayor unabashedly appropriates for himself the title of communal father, while an American mayor would not think of dramatizing his role in this way. Mayors with the characteristics described might indeed appear strange in a French context; they are, nevertheless, the most prevalent type of mayor in France.

Such mayors, however, are ridiculed as old-fashioned and retrograde by another variety of French mayor. One of the latter (a contractor) justified his qualifications for the office as follows: "Running a commune is a little like running a commercial enterprise—and I'm an entrepreneur." This second

[8] For an example, see J.-L. Quereillahc, Un tel . . . maire (Paris: Editions France-Empire, 1962), a charming and extremely informative novel about French rural mayors, pp. 24–25.
[9] For discussions of conflicting hero symbols in France, see John E. Sawyer, "Strains in the Social Structure of Modern France," in Edward M. Earle (ed.), Modern France (Princeton, N.J.: Princeton University Press, 1951), pp. 297–98; and D. W. Brogan, The Development of Modern France, II (revised ed., New York: Harper & Row, 1966), pp. 428–29.

type of mayor thinks of his commune as a business, and he likens his role to that of a manager. Compared to the images of family and father, the image of business and manager are impersonal, and imply that the goal sought is efficiency rather than warmth.[1]

Constituents rarely discussed family affairs with the mayor who styled himself a manager. If they did seek his advice, it was more likely to be in regard to governmental problems— for example, help in filling out official forms. The communal manager did not welcome intrusions by constituents; he held office hours at the town hall, and expected constituents to respect them.

Such a mayor pointed with pride to his skills as an administrator. One told how he had reorganized the communal archives. Another devoted himself to learning French administrative law, which he felt helped him in the exercise of his duties. Mayors who saw themselves as managers believed that their responsibility was to administer the commune competently; they did not feel obligated to counsel constituents on personal matters nor did they have time for purely social visits. One mayor, who was the director of a construction company, flatly stated, "I have other duties more important than being mayor." He was rarely in the commune during the day, and he did not want to devote his evenings to communal affairs.

Some mayors do not even live in the commune of which they are mayor.[2] One such mayor cited this as an advantage,

[1] Charles Roig distinguishes two types of communes on the basis of their different types of industrial development: the traditional model and the expansionist model. (See his "L'Administration locale et les changements sociaux," in Institut d'Etudes Politiques de Grenoble [ed.], Administration traditionnelle et planification régionale [Paris: Armand Colin, 1964], pp. 64–70.) Roig finds that mayors in both types of communes try to be mediators and maintain social peace; mayors in traditional communes— the great majority as Roig notes—are far more successful.

[2] Administrative law stipulates that one must merely be on the electoral or tax rolls of the commune, for example, by owning land there, in order to be eligible for election to the local government.

saying that, if he did live there, people would be continually pestering him for favors: "People come to the town hall for everything. They want advice about money, family quarrels, jobs." Another said: "For me, administering the commune isn't my major job. If I lived in the commune, I'd be bothered much more. As it is, I reserve Saturday morning for receiving anyone who wants to see me." In other words, precisely what a traditional mayor pointed to as confirmation of his prestige, another mayor regarded as an unnecessary expenditure of time. One mayor considered that the commune benefited from his living in Bordeaux rather than in the commune that he administered. By living near the prefecture and the general council, the mayor felt he was better able to protect his commune's interests: "I'm not someone who is timid and afraid to knock on the prefect's door. I'm better placed to get things done for my commune this way."[3]

Mayors who called themselves managers frequently held jobs in large enterprises. For example, one mayor was an official in a bank; another was an executive in a large wholesale food market. These were salaried officials who did not have much free time and, consequently, kept a certain distance between themselves and their elected position. While they were proud to be mayor, they nevertheless gave priority to other demands.

Unlike those mayors who saw themselves as fathers of the commune, mayors who called themselves managers did not want simply to maintain the general well-being of the community but had specific projects they sought to achieve. One mayor said indignantly: "Do you know that, until I came along, no one realized there were no public water facilities in my commune?" Another mayor described some of his fellow mayors as *petits paysans*. "They don't realize that state grants

[3] In Peyrane, however, the mayor was criticized by inhabitants because "he didn't even live in the commune . . . ." Wylie, *Village in the Vaucluse, op. cit.*, p. 173.

are there to be used. Instead, they just go along doing what the prefect tells them. That's the real *tutelle* [state supervision]. They're just like petty bureaucrats: they fill out a paper if the prefect tells them to, and that's it." The reason traditional mayors were characterized as retrogrades was precisely because they had no plans for bettering the commune. According to the more modern mayor, it was not sufficient merely to preserve the status quo; to be a good mayor meant to *improve* the facilities of the commune.

In order to sponsor local innovations, mayors are forced to ask the state for legal approval of their projects and for financial assistance. Given their goal of improving local facilities, mayors who regarded themselves as managers tried to acquire the administrative and political skills that would be helpful in their negotiations with state officials. One mayor said: "The most important thing [about being mayor] is to know where to go and how to get things done for you [by state officials]." This mayor prided himself on knowing the intricacies of the state bureaucracy. As he said, "The most plainly marked door is not always the right one; there's often a more simple one . . . in the shadows."

Because his commune is likely to be larger than the average, the mayor who compares his elected position to that of a businessman or manager often administers a commune in which managerial skills are in demand. Unlike the traditional commune, such a commune is often in process of expansion, and needs new facilities, such as schools and roads. The skills of a businessman mayor are thus necessary in order for him to administer his commune effectively. Many of the residents may have moved into the commune during or after World War II; many among them may, like their mayor, commute to work in a nearby city. These residents do not have family ties in the commune going back several generations, and they would not consider asking the mayor's advice about personal matters.

In both cases, therefore, the personality of the mayor is adapted to the character of the commune. Most French mayors, particularly in small towns, resemble one of the two types being described. Yet variations exist on the two themes. Do Communist mayors have a conception of their role that is different from that of their more conservative colleagues? One Communist mayor interviewed was indeed strikingly different from other mayors: he did not believe his role to be nonpolitical, nor did he compare his mandate to that of either a father or a manager. He was ready to admit that he appealed to a certain sector of voters and that his policies were designed to favor this group. "As a Communist, I do things differently from other mayors. . . . The principle of Communist local administration is to administer the commune in favor of the workers." However, he administered an atypical commune: more than 500 of the town's 3,300 registered voters worked in a large factory in the commune. Government officials said that Communist mayors of small rural communes were frequently indistinguishable from other mayors.[4]

Urban mayors are also different from other mayors who have been described. While a mayor of a small commune is occasionally elected to the National Assembly or the Senate, most mayors of large cities are or have been legislators.[5] (Those who are not almost invariably harbor political ambitions in this direction. Louis Pradel, mayor of Lyons, who for years has chosen not to run for national office, is an anomaly in French politics, although other examples in recent years include the mayors of Angers, Grenoble, and Toulouse.)

[4] More research on Communist mayors would be helpful. See the Communist mayors described by Gordon Wright, cited above (Footnote 4, p. 43 above), and see Chapters VI and IX below.
[5] Although France has about one-fourth the population of the United States and is far less urbanized, the French National Assembly is larger than the American House of Representatives. In most departments, there are only several cities with a population in five figures. The ratio of legislators to the general population is much higher, therefore, in France than in the United States.

Mattei Dogan has found that well over half the deputies of the Fourth Republic held local or departmental office while they were members of the National Assembly. Moreover, the proportion of deputies who were also local officeholders increased during the early years of the Fifth Republic.[6]

Non-Communist mayors of large towns seemed to synthesize elements of the two types of rural mayors. In some respects the mayor of a large town resembled the businessman mayor. He asserted, for example, that efficiency was the most important attribute needed for administering his commune properly. In choosing projects for the commune, he would maintain that he decided impartially, without favoring any group or interest over another.

A mayor of a large city was extremely busy and naturally could not know all his constituents. Yet, while legislator mayors and other mayors of large cities could not have the close relations with their constituents possible to the mayor of a small commune, this, nonetheless, seemed to be their goal. They were eager to receive requests for personal favors from constituents. Although they could not devote the major part of their time to their local mandate, they obviously considered it to be very important. And, indeed, their local mandate did help them in their primary occupation—professional politics. According to Philip M. Williams, "The town halls of France have always been a prize for politicians. They offer a platform for leadership, a source of patronage, a headquarters for a clientele and a base for a career."[7] Effective performance

---

[6] Mattei Dogan, "Changement de régime et de personnel," in Association Française de Science Politique, Le Référendum de septembre et les élections de novembre 1958 (Paris: Armand Colin, 1960), p. 259. See also Dogan, "Political Ascent in a Class Society: French Deputies 1870–1958," in Dwaine Marvick (ed.), Political Decision-makers (New York: The Free Press of Glencoe, 1961), pp. 57–90.

[7] Philip M. Williams, "Party, Presidency and Parish Pump in France," Parliamentary Affairs, XVIII (Summer 1965), 257. According to Jacques Fauvet, there exists a class of professional politicians for whom "politics is a career like any other; they advance, promoted more by seniority than by choice; they are born municipal councilors and they die senators." (Fauvet, The Cockpit of France [London: Harvill, 1960], pp. 24–25.

as mayor brought the deputy mayor votes in legislative elections. Conversely, the legislator mayor's claim to municipal office stemmed from the services he would be able to provide for his constituents as the result of his legislative position. Jacques Chaban-Delmas, mayor of Bordeaux and President of the National Assembly, illustrated the point when, during an electoral campaign, he declared, "Bordeaux needs thirty billion [*ancien*] francs to build homes. I must find these billions and not in the pockets of Bordeaux residents."[8] A legislator mayor tended to "personalize" his favors. A large city employs technical specialists, thereby freeing the mayor from technical duties. Instead of saying that he knew administrative law and the proper technical procedures, as the businessman mayor generally asserted, the deputy mayor would boast of his *personal* contacts in the government. Here one is reminded once again of the mayor who regards himself as the father of the communal family.

In large cities knowledge of the law and of technical procedures is more necessary than in small communes. Yet the mayors of large cities did not emphasize the importance of their possession of these skills.

Characteristics of the commune are thus associated with characteristics of the officeholder. In small and expanding communes, mayors are needed who have technical skills; it is these mayors who tend to consider that their task is to manage a commercial organization. Mayors of isolated rural communes, like the mayors of large cities, are more likely to be aware of the political aspect of their position.

While mayors thus differ from each other in important respects, this description of their differences is not intended to obscure the decisive respects in which their roles are similar. What unites most mayors is a common political style and a common vision of the commune. Mayors adopt a similar strategy when they attempt to achieve a change in their

[8] Quoted in Aubin, *op. cit.*, II: *Les Communes et le pays*, p. 217.

commune, and that strategy is based on their conception of how the commune should conduct its local political life. The actions of a French mayor are generally based upon a more or less explicit theory of politics; and that theory in turn is generally confirmed by his actual political activity as mayor. The mayor's importance lies in the fact that he is virtually the only person in a French commune concerned with the commune's fate. In most communes, the mayor alone decides what public facilities the local government will sponsor. One cannot mistake a mayor's paternal attitude when pointing toward "his" street-lighting or "his" municipal swimming pool.[9] And if a mayor does not foster municipal activity, public facilities in his commune are likely to be at a minimum. Local sponsorship of public facilities is the rule in France rather than the exception. Municipal governments sponsor two-thirds of all public investments in France.[1] Among a mayor's heaviest responsibilities, therefore, is the sponsorship of municipal projects.

[9] For interviews with French mayors, which illustrate the point, see *Le Monde*, March 5, 1959, March 7–8, 9, 10, 1965, and November 2, 1966; *Enterprise*, March 25, June 22, and August 31, 1963; and *Signes du temps*, March 1965.

[1] Gabriel Pallez, "L'adaptation de l'administration locale aux conditions nouvelles de la vie des cités et des communautés humaines," *Urbanisme*, XXXV (1966), 16.

THE ROLE OF FRENCH LOCAL GOVERNMENT

PART II

THE ROLE OF
FRENCH LOCAL
GOVERNMENT

Chapter III

Initiative for Local Innovations

𝕏 Much of a French local government's activity is routine: one would not expect controversy to erupt over the registration of new voters, the maintenance of the local school, or the collection of refuse. Although conflict appears more likely when a local government undertakes a new project, the way in which local governments sponsor innovations is also designed to preserve the appearance of communal harmony. An examination of how local innovations are proposed illustrates the painstaking process by which change is instituted in order to maintain stability.

When the initiative for a project originates with anyone in the commune, that person is likely to be the mayor. For example, in the commune studied by Roger Josserand, only the mayor, assistant mayor, and town clerk were involved in the commune's political life.[1] However, since mayors are generally unwilling to risk possible controversy and are for the most

---

[1] Roger Josserand, "Rapport d'enquête sur la commune de Marigny en Charolais" (Unpublished Mémoire, Institut d'Etudes Politiques de Grenoble, n.d.), p. 9. The French attitude toward participation in local government may not be unique. See comments on this question by citizens of several countries in Gabriel A. Almond and Sidney Verba, *The Civic Culture* (Boston: Little, Brown, 1964), pp. 131-32.

part inclined toward conservatism, national government officials also try to instigate municipal action.

In the most comprehensive study to date of French pressure groups, Jean Meynaud notes that pressure group activity at the local level "is an unknown subject. In France, the question has not been the object of systematic study."[2] It would appear that relatively few organizations exist within a commune that might press for local governmental action. Orvoell R. Gallagher found a total of fifteen voluntary associations in a French rural commune of 800 inhabitants. He concludes:

Not only are associations few in number, but they seldom play a vital role in community life. The few existing associations . . . could, in this writer's opinion, be eliminated from community life without much effect on the daily life of the inhabitants.[3]

Mayors reported receiving occasional suggestions from constituents for major projects—for example, a day nursery. But such demands were infrequent and, even then, rarely organized. Ridley and Blondel note that "a mayor with a strong personality often dominates the life of his commune. Together with his assistant mayors . . . he is the originator of most proposals and schemes. . . ."[4]

[2] Jean Meynaud, Nouvelles études sur les groupes de pression en France (Paris: Armand Colin, 1962), p. 284.

[3] Orvoell R. Gallagher, "Voluntary Associations in France," Social Forces, XXXVI (December 1957), 155. However, quite likely, there has been a proliferation of voluntary associations locally. In a private communication, Laurence Wylie states, "I think the growth of voluntary associations has been phenomenal." See also Alain Barrère, "Société démocratique et société urbanisée," in Semaines Sociales de France (ed.), L'Homme et la révolution urbaine (Lyons: Chronique Sociale de France, 1965), pp. 335–55; Edward Tannenbaum, The New France (Chicago: University of Chicago Press, 1961), pp. 8–9; Gordon Wright, Rural Revolution in France (Stanford, Calif.: Stanford University Press, 1964); Laurence Wylie (ed.), Chanzeaux: A Village in Anjou (Cambridge: Harvard University Press, 1966), Chap. 11; and the discussions of dépolitisation in France, in Colloque 'France Forum' (ed.), La Démocratie à refaire (Paris: Les Editions Ouvrières, 1963); and Georges Vedel (ed.), La Dépolitisation: mythe ou réalité? (Paris: Armand Colin, 1962).

[4] F. Ridley and J. Blondel, Public Administration in France (London: Routledge & Kegan Paul, Ltd., 1964), p. 95.

One mayor replied, when asked if groups in the commune made proposals to the local government, "That's the [local] government's task, isn't it?" Inhabitants of a commune are not accustomed to creating organizations for the purpose of enlisting the local government's support.[5]

Since most communes are small, citizens might participate directly in local governmental decisions. In many communes one might dispense with the municipal council altogether and decide important questions at a meeting of the commune's citizens. The obvious possibility of a town meeting, however, has virtually never been even discussed in France.[6] French administrative law even goes so far as to forbid communes to hold referendums on local questions. It is illegal for a municipal council to sponsor a formal referendum on an issue under consideration, even if the referendum does not bind the municipal council and is simply intended to elicit communal opinion.[7]

The reluctance of the French to encourage popular participation in government was manifested in a Catholic-sponsored colloquium that examined the bases for a democratic society. In July 1963 the fiftieth *Semaine Sociale de France* was held at Caen, bringing together scholars, laymen, govern-

[5] Local governments, however, give financial grants to organizations within the commune. After observing municipal council meetings in which applications for grants were presented, my impression is that all groups that ask receive at least nominal sums.

[6] For an exception—a brief discussion over one-half century ago of municipal referendums—see Charles Bellangé, *Le gouvernement local en France et l'organisation du canton* (Paris: Didier, 1900), pp. 113–18. See also Roger Aubin, *Communes et démocratie, II: les communes et le pays* (Paris: Les Editions Ouvrières, 1965), pp. 34–35.

[7] However, if the fusion of several communes is proposed, the local sub-prefect may hold a referendum on the question in the communes involved. To illustrate French governmental opposition to direct participation: when Germany occupied Alsace-Lorraine in the late nineteenth century, she decreed that in very small communes the municipal council would be formed of the entire electorate. After France regained control of the area, she replaced the system by the traditional French method of electing municipal councils. (Jean-Daniel Herrenschmidt, "Le problème des petites communes en France" [unpublished thesis, University of Paris, Faculty of Law, 1936], p. 29.)

ment officials, clergymen, and representatives of professional groups. One panel, made up of municipal councilors and citizens, discussed French municipal life and, in particular, how the municipal council could be made more responsive to citizen opinion. The following suggestions for new forms of representation emerged from these discussions:

1. letters from citizens to the municipal council
2. conferences between the mayor and leaders of interest groups in the commune
3. para-municipal council commissions, composed of municipal councilors and citizens, which would be concerned with functions of municipal administration, such as roads, education, and sports
4. a requirement that municipal councilors give explanations of municipal council decisions to citizens
5. *action directe*.[8]

Although most of these practices would be taken for granted by an American, participants at the conference regarded them as innovations in communal political life. True, even an American might shy away from recommending *action directe*—until he learned that what was intended was not revolutionary action directed against the local government, but rather petitions that citizens might address to the municipal council!

An article by a former French mayor, in which he advocates greater "direct democracy," also demonstrates a curious definition of the term: the author suggests that municipal councilors should have more frequent contact with constituents "in order to inform citizens of existing problems and of *the*

[8] *La Semaine sociale de Caen,* Results of the Commission on Municipal Life, July 10, 1963. See also Maurice Flory, "La Démocratie dans le cadre local et régional," in the collection of speeches made at *La Semaine Sociale de Caen, La Société démocratique* (Paris: Sirey, 1963), pp. 241–59.

manner in which the local government intends to resolve them.[9]

Those rare occasions when citizens participate directly in the political life of their commune are considered worthy of special note. An article in a Socialist publication praises citizen participation in para-municipal council commissions of a commune with 360 voters.[1]

Another logical source from which initiatives for communal projects might originate is the municipal council. Yet the municipal council rarely serves this purpose. One municipal councilor stated simply, "No, the municipal council doesn't do much. We usually follow the mayor's advice." Mayors agreed that the municipal council followed their direction rather than originating ideas. One observer suggests that the municipal council's role is usually "limited to the absolute minimum: the sole moving force is the mayor. He alone analyzes local problems, takes the initiative for projects . . . and, when he judges opportune, informs the municipal council of a project he has conceived."[2]

At municipal council meetings councilors transmit a variety of suggestions to the mayor. For example, at a municipal council meeting in one commune the following problems were indicated to the mayor:

1. a street lamp had burned out
2. a stop sign was needed at a particular intersection
3. garbage from a neighboring commune was being dumped in the commune, causing an unpleasant smell and a health hazard
4. the town clock was running slow.

[9] Jacques Madaule, "Quatre ans de mairie," *Esprit*, XXI (May 1953), 782. Italics mine.
[1] Roger Beaunez, "Une expérience où on fait confiance," *Perspectives socialistes* (January 1963). See also Aubin, *op. cit.*, II, pp. 37–42.
[2] Charles Schmitt, *Le Maire de la commune rurale* (Paris: Berger-Levrault, 1959), p. 46. See also Wylie (ed.), *Chanzeaux, op. cit.*, pp. 228–29.

However, rather than constituting demands for important innovations in the commune, these requests resemble the favors that constituents ask directly of their mayor.

When municipal councilors themselves are asked who originates communal projects, they invariably reply that it is the mayor who is responsible. According to government officials, however, this judgment is false: projects frequently originate in state bureaus. Administrators provide the mayor with the impetus to undertake many governmental projects. Officials are instructed by their superiors which projects the government favors so they can encourage communes to undertake those projects. Financial grants are offered to make government-favored projects appear particularly attractive. For example, the government has tried to ensure that all Frenchmen are provided with public water facilities. In areas without a public system of water distribution subprefects are asked to persuade communes to sponsor these facilities, for which the state will subsidize up to 85 per cent of the cost. Since small communes do not have a large enough population to make such a system feasible, the normal procedure is for several communes to form an intercommunal association to share the costs of the undertaking. A subprefect related that he had attended cantonal meetings of mayors or had visited mayors individually, encouraging them to join an association. Despite the advantages of a communal water supply, mayors were reluctant to join the association. One reason is that they were afraid local independence would be compromised. One mayor replied, when asked if he would sponsor the fusion of his tiny commune with a neighboring commune, "We want nothing to do with foreigners."[3] Moreover, no grant-in-aid

---

[3] Quoted in Wright, *op. cit.*, p. 15 note, from *La revue administrative.* For an account of the considerable efforts a subprefect was required to expend to launch an intercommunal project, see Roger Vignaud, "Le sous-préfet dans un arrondissement rural," *Etude des problèmes municipaux*, no. 6 (June 1965), 28–32. Also see J.-L. Quereillahc, *Un tel . . . maire* (Paris: France-Empire, 1962), p. 120.

completely covers the cost of a local project. Since local governments must assume part of the cost, and since they are suspicious of state advice, efforts by state officials are not assured of success.[4]

Technical ministries of the national government also have representatives in the department.[5] A mayor provided evidence of the influence possessed by one specialized agency, the Rural Engineers Corps (*Génie Rural*). The local rural engineer circulated a questionnaire to mayors asking about their communes' water needs.[6] The communes wanted water but, because each was small, it was necessary to form an association that grouped the communes into one joint water system. None of the mayors in the region had suggested forming an intercommunal association for joint water distribution. The mayor interviewed ascribed complete responsibility for the undertaking to the local rural engineer.

After making an estimate of the communes' needs, the rural engineer studied the technical possibilities of the proposal and told the mayors involved that he would advise them of the results. According to the mayor, "If the Rural Engineers Corps approves the project, the district engineer will convoke the mayors in the area to tell them of the decision." In brief,

---

[4] A rural mayor, Ernest Monpied, describes the difficult and controversial process by which *remembrement* (regrouping of scattered farmland into larger parcels) was accomplished in his commune. (Monpied, *Terres mouvantes, un maire rural au coeur du remembrement* [Paris: Les Editions Ouvrières, 1965].) The local subprefect suggested the commune undertake the arduous project; he was able to secure municipal council approval only by promising to obtain the government's authorization for a pending local proposal. (*Ibid.*, pp. 13–14.) A study of rural mayors finds that they hesitate proposing *remembrement* because of the "risk that it may engender opposition." (Thierry de Beaucé, "Opinions et attitudes des maires ruraux," [unpublished Mémoire, Institut d'Etudes Politiques de Paris, 1964], p. 80.)

[5] For a discussion of the activity of the specialized ministries in the provinces, see Brian Chapman, *The Prefects and Provincial France* (London: George Allen & Unwin, 1955), Chap. 4.

[6] One of the functions of the Rural Engineers Corps is to give technical assistance to communes which are planning municipal water facilities.

the process was described as if the national government were empowered to force local sponsorship, although by law the state cannot force a commune to undertake a project: communes undertake projects at their own discretion.

The example cited suggests how field services use their expertise and financial resources to influence local decisions. In a similar fashion, Jean Blondel describes Rural Engineers Corps activity in the Eure-et-Loir. After the service has prepared a technical plan:

The engineer will most probably address the [municipal council] meeting, explain details, giving reasons why, for instance, he favours a given solution rather than another. He will, in fact, have to convince the Council but that is supposed to be easy in Eure-et-Loir. He might threaten a recalcitrant Council by saying that if the commune is not prepared to accept the proposals, he would be only too pleased, his office being already overcrowded.[7]

Jean-Pierre Worms has described a new type of French public official who is particularly interested in stimulating public investments. One bureau chief explained to him that if a commune is inactive:

. . . the subprefect makes a suggestion to the mayor. We also encourage the intervention of the technical services (particularly the Ingénieur des Ponts et Chaussées [Engineer of Bridges and Roads]) who have a great influence on municipalities. This role of impulsion is very new. Until recently, we merely abided by what the commune decided.[8]

---

[7] J. Blondel, "Local Government and the Ministries in a French *Département*," *Public Administration* (London), XXXVII (Spring 1959), 71. Blondel's article traces the historical and technical reasons for the relative inactivity of French local governments. He suggests that, even in matters that are local responsibilities, state technical services frequently govern directly rather than through the local government.

[8] Jean-Pierre Worms, of the Institut de Sociologie Européenne, kindly made available notes of interviews conducted with officials of the prefecture of Beauvais (Oise). See his forthcoming study of prefectural officials and his article, "Le Préfet et ses notables," *Sociologie du Travail*, VIII (July–September 1966), 249–75. (M. Worms' interview notes will hereafter be cited as "Worms interviews.")

Another bureaucrat explained, "We have an important role in initiating projects . . . Localities are always ready to accept the suggestions of the prefecture."[9]

A study of small communes in the Manche finds that activity there is usually generated by state officials. Several of the prefecture's bureau chiefs and the chief of the Division of Communal Affairs spend one-fourth of their time giving advice to mayors in regard to local projects. State officials may also stimulate local projects more actively, for example, when the prefect addresses meetings of mayors.[1]

The persuasive powers of the prefect may be very great indeed. One mayor in the Calvados described why he agreed to authorize a ZUP (*zone à urbaniser en priorité*) in his commune.[2] Before the ZUP was undertaken, the commune over which the mayor presided had 1,700 inhabitants. In several years, the commune would undergo a total transformation, with its population scheduled to attain 32,000. According to the mayor, he gave his consent only because the prefect had convinced him that the project was essential to regional growth. The decision to sponsor the project created enormous problems for the mayor whose task it was to justify and gain acceptance for the undertaking. The mayor admitted that the proposal was extremely unpopular in his commune. Farmers were bitterly opposed because they would be forced to sell their land to make way for the project. "Luckily, they didn't have a majority on the municipal council," he said, "but I still had to threaten to resign before the council approved the proposal."[3]

---

[9] *Ibid.*
[1] Pierre Bandet, "L'Avenir des petites communes de la Manche" (unpublished Mémoire, Ecole Nationale d'Administration, Paris, 1958).
[2] This is a new form of land development, similar to urban renewal projects in the United States, which permits land to be used for a variety of purposes. State grants and private investments are pooled, and a number of projects are undertaken within a given area.
[3] In Monpied, *op. cit.*, pp. 166–69, a rural mayor recounts how he threatens to resign as mayor when a local project he is sponsoring encounters opposition in the commune.

Sponsoring a local project and obtaining the requisite state approvals, loans, and financial grants is a long and tedious process.[4] In order to apply for a grant, a commune whose professional staff may consist of one part-time town clerk is required to submit detailed technical forms. The state bureaucracy works extremely slowly: years elapse between the application for a state grant and the commune's receipt of the actual funds. Since sponsoring a communal improvement involves many such difficulties, what impels mayors to undertake local projects?

Mayors undertake projects for reasons similar to those that impel them to become mayors in the first place. One mayor told of "wanting to do something for my commune." Although he had a successful insurance practice, he felt an obligation to improve his commune. "In twenty-five years, my insurance business will be mostly the same. But if I can look around my commune and see a school that I built, or a park, then I'll feel proud." Another mayor remarked indignantly, "You know, when I was elected mayor [in 1952], there wasn't even a municipal water system, and we're only eight kilometers from Bordeaux. The previous mayor hadn't even thought of putting one in."

A prefect's chief aide said, "They [the mayors] have a *domaine réservé* where they're all-powerful dictators. It is the only elected function where one can really accomplish something."[5] A former cabinet minister remarked, "Being mayor is the only way politicians can satisfy their thirst for action."[6]

In interviews, mayors described in language strikingly reminiscent of that used by the late President Kennedy what induced them to undertake projects. One said, "The region is in full development and we don't want to be left behind";

---

[4] However, as will be discussed in succeeding chapters, much of the work mayors do in this regard is self-imposed.
[5] De Beaucé interviews.
[6] Robert Buron, *Le Plus beau des métiers* (Paris: Plon, 1963), p. 95.

another asserted, "You can't stay in one place. Either you go forward or you fall back."

Mayors sponsor local innovations that will bring the commune closer to their vision of what it should be. For example, the national government had decreed that the age for leaving school was to be raised from fourteen to sixteen. While local governments were previously required to provide educational facilities for all children up to age fourteen in the commune, henceforth additional facilities would be needed to accommodate the fourteen-to-sixteen age group. One way to meet the new requirement would have been simply to enlarge the existing schools in all communes. However, one mayor discussed why he decided to help form an intercommunal association which would sponsor a new central school and school-bus transportation. The mayor confided that he felt the additional expense and change in traditional practices advisable because of the age of the youngsters affected by the new requirement. Since a great many students would attend the central school, classes would be divided by sex, as they are traditionally in large schools in France. If each commune were simply to enlarge its existing facilities, however, all of the pupils would be in the same room; adolescents of both sexes would be thrown into close proximity. "And," he muttered darkly, "who knows with children of that age if we might not have a case of pregnancy on our hands?"

Thus, the mayor reluctantly agreed to join an intercommunal association in order to preserve the moral purity of the commune's youth. While the step represented an important innovation in the commune's political and social habits, the mayor agreed to the change because he felt that it was necessary in order to maintain the commune's traditional values.[7]

[7] One might distinguish mayors according to the reasons they furnished for undertaking projects. The classification resembles the one suggested in the previous chapter. Father-mayors undertake projects to preserve the traditional values of the commune; businessman-mayors undertake projects to modernize their commune.

Another mayor recognized that communal improvements were needed if his commune were not to diminish in size. He was concerned about the commune's future and wanted to ensure that its size and character would be maintained. He told sadly of how the population of his tiny commune had diminished from 177 to 168 inhabitants in the past eight years. While several laborers from other areas of France had moved to the commune, the sons of old farming families in the area had moved to Caen or Paris. He was concerned that, unless work and entertainment facilities were available in the commune, even more young people would leave. However, this mayor was unusual in his recognition of the influence that local government might have on communal development.[8] While, admittedly, communes have to contend with the highly centralized French administrative system and with severe financial limitations, local governments are able to sponsor a wide variety of communal innovations. Nonetheless, most French communes contain a minimum of public facilities. Until recently, it was not unusual to find communes without electricity and running water. While such basic facilities are now widespread, the same is not true for other amenities. Few communes provide sports fields, public parks, municipal nurseries, public baths, or school-bus transportation.

Perhaps the critical question, therefore, is not why mayors undertake projects but why they undertake so few of them. (According to Brian Chapman, "The real question is not that they [local governments] are inefficient in what they do, but that they do not do nearly enough."[9]) One answer might be that the lack of organized pressure within the commune which permits mayors to monopolize initiatives for local reforms also permits them not to act at all. Sponsoring a project is an

[8] The mayor in Quereillahc's novel also sees the connection between the local government and the commune's declining population (op. cit., p. 192).
[9] Brian Chapman, An Introduction to French Local Government (London: George Allen & Unwin, 1953), p. 225.

arduous undertaking, often not in the immediate interests of the mayor—who, moreover, is not paid. Unlike most elected officials, mayors do not have to compile favorable records in order to increase their chances for re-election. Unless they are grossly incompetent, the chances are high that they will be re-elected.

As undisputed leader of the commune, the mayor retains the power to decide which communal projects will best serve communal ends.[1] Yet, because he views community harmony as the overriding end, he is unwilling to sponsor controversial projects. Any important communal change is likely to affect local groups in different ways—which in turn will weaken local unity. Consequently, mayors choose projects which are not controversial, and most local governments have relatively conservative policies. Communal harmony is strengthened by the fact that, within the commune, the local government—meaning the mayor—retains exclusive power to initiate local reforms. But the mayor's power and the commune's harmony are purchased at a price.

[1] The process is similar in Japanese village government. "Since almost all by-laws [the equivalent of French municipal council deliberations] are proposed by the mayor, the process greatly favors his predominance." (Kurt Steiner, "The Japanese Village and Its Government," *Far Eastern Quarterly*, XV [February 1956], 190.) See the symposium on "Village Government in Eastern and Southern Asia," in the February 1956 issue of the *Far Eastern Quarterly*, and particularly the Introduction by Robert Ward, for interesting comparisons with French local government.

Chapter IV

The Manufacture of Consent

Because the mayor is eager to maintain unanimity on local matters, once he has decided to sponsor a project he takes particular care to secure the consent of the important forces in his commune. Chief among these is the municipal council.

Like any political institution, the municipal council has both a legal existence and an informal life. In French administrative law, the municipal council has responsibility for all matters of local concern; the mayor is required to execute municipal council deliberations. Yet the actual position of the municipal council cannot be ascertained from a description of its extensive legal powers.

According to Robert Arambourou, in the area he studied the typical mayor "resembles a veritable local potentate in the midst of his council of elders and vassals. . . ."[1]

Most of the mayors interviewed did not have a high opinion of their municipal councils, although none were as blunt as one mayor in the Dordogne who growled, "A municipal councilor isn't worth a damn."[2]

[1] Robert Arambourou, "La Gavacherie de Montségur," in François Goguel (ed.), *Nouvelles études de sociologie électorale* (Paris: Armand Colin, 1954), p. 113.
[2] De Beaucé interviews.

In Salignac, capital of a canton in the Dordogne, one observer noted that "the commune is directed by the mayor and the assistant mayor. The others [on the municipal council] follow. No opposition, no assistance, and, of course, no tension."[3] A study of a rural commune reports that the municipal council "is there only as a matter of form and because it is required by law."[4] The author notes that the municipal council "corresponds to no useful reality." Instead, it simply formalizes decisions already made by the mayor, the town clerk, and the assistant mayor.

Ridley and Blondel conclude that the municipal council is:

. . . weak vis-à-vis the mayor and the central administration. . . . The council does not play the leading part in local government except where the mayor is a weak personality or lacks firm political support in the council.[5]

Several mayors furnished a clear illustration of the status of the municipal council when they disclosed that the mayor is permitted to act in the name of the municipal council even without the council having voted him proper authorization. As described by one mayor, "A deliberation is sent to the prefecture [without having actually been voted on by the municipal council]. Then, later, the councilors are presented with a *fait accompli* and they sign their names to the official

---

[3] J.-P. Faucounau, "L'Evolution des communautés locales," *Construire*, No. 56 (July 1962), p. 22. The author contrasts the local government of Salignac with the local government of another commune in a more dynamic department (the Eure). However, even the municipal council in the latter commune does not appear active or independent.

Younger mayors may be changing traditional practice by working more closely with their municipal councilors. See Laurence Wylie (ed.), *Chanzeaux: A Village in Anjou* (Cambridge: Harvard University Press, 1966), pp. 238–39.

[4] Roger Josserand, "Rapport d'enquête sur la commune de Marigny en Charolais" (unpublished Mémoire, Institut d'Etudes Politiques de Grenoble, n.d.), p. 9.

[5] F. Ridley and J. Blondel, *Public Administration in France* (London: Routledge & Kegan Paul, Ltd., 1964), p. 98.

register." Thus, the municipal council passes a deliberation that legalizes an action the mayor has *already* performed.

One writer suggests that the real responsibility for this fairly common practice lies with the national government. When the prefect or subprefect stipulates that a municipal council deliberation is needed in order to regularize a mayoral action, he telephones the mayor. The mayor, in turn, fictively "remembers" that the municipal council has indeed deliberated on the matter in question. He has the town clerk transcribe the deliberation onto the official register of deliberations, and he then sends the "corrected" register to the prefecture or subprefecture.[6] Upon being asked if he considered the procedure legal, one mayor replied reproachfully, "But there's nothing wrong with it. It's much easier than calling a meeting —and besides, if my councilors were opposed, I wouldn't do it."[7]

One mayor explained why municipal councilors rarely demonstrate qualities of leadership:

Elderly councilors leave speaking to the mayor. And the young councilor is obliged to keep quiet out of respect for his colleagues. Why should he, more than they, have the right to entertain a clear idea on the obscure problem being discussed?[8]

A municipal councilor defined the council's role as follows: "We listen to the mayor's ideas and try to help him with his task." Councilors do not picture the local government as a small-scale reproduction of the national government, with the mayor as executive and the municipal council as legislature,

[6] Charles Schmitt, *Le Maire de la commune rurale* (Paris: Berger-Levrault, 1959), pp. 46–47.

[7] What is significant about the mayor's statement is not that he is wrong but what his being right implies about the municipal council. For a case where a mayor was removed from office, allegedly for political reasons, after such an infraction, see *Le Monde*, April 6, 1967.

[8] Cited in Thierry de Beaucé, "Opinions et attitudes des maires ruraux" (unpublished Mémoire, Institut d'Etudes Politiques de Paris, 1964), pp. 86–87. The statement points to an unexplored area where research would be fruitful: the apprenticeship preceding the mayor's emergence as leader.

exercising a check on executive power. They do not believe a functional division exists between mayor and municipal council but rather a sort of partnership—with the latter in the decidedly subordinate role.

The municipal council's lack of vitality, as reported by scholars, municipal councilors, and mayors is particularly evident at municipal council meetings. Attending these meetings reinforces the impression that the council does not play a significant role in shaping the commune's political life. The mayor dominates the discussion. His physical location symbolizes his superiority to others on the municipal council. He may sit on a raised platform, at the head of the table, or, according to one observer, alone at the municipal council table—with the other councilors seated respectfully at the perimeter of the room.[9]

On rare occasions councilors publicly differed with their mayor, but not a single case was observed in which they successfully convinced their colleagues. Whereas the mayor was familiar with all matters on the agenda, those who differed with him were poorly informed—as were, indeed, most of the municipal councilors. Many councilors appeared not even to have read the dossiers under discussion until they arrived at the meeting. The mayor conferred constantly with the town clerk and with technical specialists, but these officials did not assist councilors.

In one canton, when there are discussions at municipal council meetings:

One concludes by reaching agreement en famille—nearly unanimously: voting rarely occurs. Significantly, at these times the mayor emerges with even greater personal authority—for he can say to the men that complain, "It is the council that decided." Still more significant, final agreement is nearly always realized in

[9] Bernard Gournay, "Seminaire sur les administrations françaises" (unpublished notes, Library of the Foundation Nationale des Sciences Politiques, Paris, 1962).

regard to a project and on a motion which originated with the mayor himself.[1]

At one municipal council meeting a heated discussion broke out between several councilors and the mayor about the accuracy of the minutes reporting a decision made at the previous meeting. When the mayor was questioned, he quickly denied responsibility for the minutes and said that any mistake was the town clerk's fault. Then, when criticism did not abate, he angrily adjourned the meeting for ten minutes, stating that, when the meeting resumed, he would immediately pass on to the next item on the agenda. With this, the mayor stalked out of the room, leaving behind a grumbling group of powerless councilors.

At a municipal council meeting in another commune the mayor asked the municipal council to authorize a large sum of money for the expansion of the municipal slaughterhouse facilities. The mayor, the assistant mayor concerned with the project, and the town clerk presented a detailed proposal which the municipal council had no choice but to accept. The matter was formally concluded within minutes, although it appeared that the municipal councilors barely had time to scrutinize the proposal.

Most municipal council meetings appear similar to those held in Vienne:

Meetings of the municipal council are conducted according to a strict drum-beat. Opening the meeting at the exact time—the city's chief executive doesn't tolerate tardiness—he quickly reads the motions on the agenda, with councilors, "program" in hand, trying to follow. Votes are taken so rapidly it isn't certain that everyone knows what he is voting for; sometimes hands are raised on the "offbeat," after a motion. A councilor belonging to the opposition tries to intervene. Because he has misunderstood what he read too fast or because he doesn't have sufficient documenta-

[1] Eric Degremont, "Les Maires ruraux, leur autorité" (unpublished Mémoire, Institut d'Etudes Politiques de Paris, 1965), p. 46. See also de Beaucé, *op. cit.*, p. 88.

tion or eloquence, he is soon reduced to silence by a precise and penetrating reply from the mayor, who closes the discussion by "Agreed?"—more commanding than questioning. The meeting is adjourned as nimbly as it began. . . . Such is the traditional procedure of this "obligatory ceremony." . . .[2]

Councilors do not appear to be disturbed about municipal council inactivity. At one municipal meeting, a councilor apologized profusely when he presented a carefully prepared criticism of a municipally sponsored housing project. Nor do mayors either expect or encourage municipal council debate. One mayor stated flatly, "If there's too much time taken up [at municipal council meetings] by endless discussion and stupidity, then I'll just quit."

Only occasionally is there municipal council opposition to the local government. For example, a councilor from Bordeaux wrote a bitter letter to the local newspaper protesting that a pamphlet describing the Bordeaux trade fair had been widely distributed without "ever having been shown to the municipal councilors who belong to the opposition. It's the same for all important projects. We're asked either to accept or refuse expenditures, without being given any information about the proposal."[3] Structured opposition arose only when there was a minority viewpoint represented on the municipal council—and was generally confined to the largest cities, such as Bordeaux, where the municipal council had been elected according to proportional representation in the 1959 local elections. In smaller cities, when lists of candidates were formed in opposition to the incumbent administration, the electoral system made it difficult for candidates from opposition lists to gain election. The abolition of proportional representation in 1965 and the system of blocked lists in cities

[2] Pierre Clément and Nelly Xydias, *Vienne sur le Rhône* (Paris: Armand Colin, 1955), pp. 131–32. See also Wylie (ed.), *Chanzeaux, op. cit.*, p. 228.
[3] Letter to the *Sud-Ouest* (Bordeaux), March 31, 1963, by Dr. Castets, municipal councilor of Bordeaux.

over 30,000 further minimized the chance of minority representation on the municipal council.

The municipal council does not exercise the dominant role in communal affairs provided for it by French administrative law; rather it performs its legal duties in a perfunctory fashion.

As the commune's legislature, the council is woefully deficient. Even in large communes the municipal council does not possess a technical staff to assist it in examining executive proposals. And councilors are unable by themselves to scrutinize competently mayoral policies and the actions of municipal officials. The municipal council does not govern the commune, nor does it actively scrutinize executive actions. However, it would be false to conclude that, because the municipal council does not exercise its legal powers vigorously, it is thereby an insignificant element in French local politics.

When mayors say that the municipal council is unimportant, they refer to the way in which it exercises its formal responsibilities. But, although mayors point out that the municipal council does not function as it should, this does not mean that they ignore the important place the council actually occupies in the commune. Mayors go out of their way to ensure council support for their projects. The mayor of one commune observed, "The municipal council doesn't like to make decisions."[4] Consequently, he said that he was obliged to visit his councilors as well as the *"grands électeurs—* those who count, whether [political] friends or adversaries,"* in order to gain support for his policies.

One mayor confided, "It's a delicate matter, the municipal council. Councilors don't want to work, but if they're not consulted about a project they feel slighted. One must try to balance the two."

The typical mayor has little reason to fear the formal power of the municipal council. It is doubtful that the council

---

[4] Philippe Lamirault, "Le Maire rural," in Gournay, *op. cit.*

will refuse to authorize policies proposed by the mayor. Even more unlikely would be the municipal council's resigning in protest against the mayor's policies.[5] Yet in the mayor's conception of communal life, the municipal council is seen as not only representing, but standing for—taking the place of—the commune. What the mayor strives for is not merely the municipal council's assent, which he will probably obtain in any event; his aim is to secure its united and willing assent. If the council is unanimously and actively satisfied with mayoral decisions, this signifies that the commune is ideally united.[6]

The municipal council's function is thus primarily symbolic. A mayor does not expect or desire the council to function as a legislative body; rather, he wants the municipal council to ratify decisions that he has already reached, and he wants council ratifications to place the commune enthusiastically behind its mayor. What the mayor aims for is that the municipal council, as a "council of elders and vassals," should fully endorse his decisions. The function of the municipal council is thus to provide formal expression to the informal consensus prevailing in the commune. For this purpose the municipal council is ideal.[7]

[5] In An Introduction to French Local Government (London: George Allen & Unwin, 1953), pp. 35–36, Brian Chapman implies that these cases are fairly frequent. Far more usual is for the mayor and municipal council together to demonstrate or even resign against the national government's policies. For some examples, see Jean Meynaud, Les Groupes de pression en France (Paris: Armand Colin, 1958), p. 155.

[6] See Part Three for a fuller discussion of this issue. In small communities in the United States, Grant McConnell finds that "the goal sought is usually much more than establishment of a majority; it is likely to be utter unanimity." (McConnell, Private Power and American Democracy [New York: Alfred A. Knopf, 1966], p. 349.) In East and South Asian villages, Robert Ward stresses "the extent of reliance upon popular consensus as the means of taking important local decisions." (Ward, "Introduction: Village Government in Eastern and Southern Asia," Far Eastern Quarterly, XV [February 1956], 181.) Kurt Steiner also notes that, in Japanese village council meetings, "the appearance of conformity is highly valued. . . ." ("The Japanese Village and Its Government," ibid., p. 190.) See also Steiner, Local Government in Japan (Stanford, Calif.: Stanford University Press, 1965), p. 211.

[7] One important reason is the municipal council's composition, which will be examined in Chapter VIII.

One mayor remarked:

This is a difficult time because of the period of expansion we're experiencing. We need to have water, routes, and amenities. . . . Therefore, I must work together with the municipal council. It's better to involve as many men as possible in the decisions reached because that diminishes opposition. Above all, we must do this to avoid a systematic opposition.[8]

The typical procedure that mayors follow is to secure their councilors' assent individually for a local project before the municipal council is asked to give its formal approval. Mayors employ different methods to inform councilors. Several mayors told of calling an informal meeting every several weeks with their assistant mayors and influential councilors, where agreement was reached on the major projects pending. Subsequent discussion of these issues at council meetings therefore had little real importance. At Nouville a similar procedure is followed. "Before the rural constable delivers the notice of a municipal council meeting to the councilors, the mayor tours the commune by automobile in order [according to the town clerk] 'to visit his pals [on the municipal council].' "[9]

By carefully developing their support before a project is formally proposed, mayors attempt to avoid even the possibility of controversy. And projects that are likely to become controversial or may redound to the mayor's disadvantage are not even proposed. At Vienne, "when the mayor does not have sufficient votes [in the municipal council] to pass a project, he prefers to let it drop altogether rather than to lose face by being in the minority."[1]

[8] "Systematic opposition" means an organized opposition in local elections.
[9] Lucien Bernot and René Blancard, *Nouville, un village français* (Travaux et Mémoires de l'Institut d'Ethnologie, LVII; University of Paris, 1953), p. 243.
[1] Clément and Xydias, *op. cit.*, p. 133. At Vienne, with the system of proportional representation for local elections at that time, opposition lists were represented on the municipal council. After 1959 the opposition stood a far smaller chance of even being elected to the municipal council, much less of overruling the mayor.

A town clerk complained about his mayor, denouncing what he considered to be the mayor's "devious and continual maneuverings." The clerk said that the mayor was interested only in gaining personal support: he did not adopt policies because they were intrinsically desirable, but merely because they would increase his popularity. The clerk asserted that the mayor was not interested in such important duties as registering young men for the draft, preparing the electoral list, and registering births and deaths. The only comparable function that attracted the mayor was performing marriages—because many residents of the commune attended the ceremony, providing the mayor with a chance to receive considerable attention![2] The town clerk angrily related how the mayor was primarily interested in granting favors and getting support for his projects. He criticized the mayor for "playing politics."

One major reason why mayors "play politics" is to unite their communes for defense against the outside world. In particular, a divided commune feels itself to be in a weak position to manipulate the state; yet the state must be "conquered" before the commune can expect help in improving its public facilities. The state's legal approval and financial support are required and, it is believed, will not be forthcoming without a struggle. The image is a martial one: the state will have to be vanquished or, probably more accurately, manipulated before the commune can get what it wants. It is thereby assumed that there is a conflict of interest between the state and the commune. Consequently, the commune must take care to be in the best defensive position; if it is not, it may itself be duped.

The rationale for a united commune thus takes on even greater force. If the commune does not present a united visage,

[2] The film *Carnet de Bal* portrays a wedding ceremony where the bridegroom (Raimu)—the commune's mayor—officiates at his own marriage, with the commune's residents in enthusiastic attendance. (The lamentable and pedantic reality is that the ceremony would be held invalid according to French law.)

it will be especially susceptible to the state's wiles. A mayor must take particular care to preserve local consensus when he embarks on a project that requires state involvement, for that is when the commune is at its most vulnerable.

The mayor must, therefore, utilize every possible source of assistance in his encounter with the state. It is in this struggle between state and commune that parliamentary representatives can render their greatest service to the commune. Acquainted with the arcane operations of the distant state, they are at the same time elected to represent the commune's interests. Enlisting legislators' support is a critical step in the struggle to outwit the state.

Chapter V

Enlisting Legislators' Support

Mayors frequently require assistance from the national government for their municipal projects. A mayor believes that, since the state will not act according to the merits of a case, it is, therefore, incumbent on him to use all available help. According to one mayor, "The ministries [in Paris] won't listen to us unless we're influential or politically friendly." Because mayors picture the government as unwilling to provide assistance voluntarily, they believe adherence to an informal ritual is necessary. "The typical mayor conceives of a grant not as assistance accorded by law but as a favor graciously bestowed by a faraway and benevolent authority. . . ."[1] Enlisting the support of elected representatives is a necessary precaution preparatory to confronting the national government.

Legislators, in turn, sometimes go to extraordinary lengths to demonstrate support for the commune in its struggle with

[1] Thierry de Beaucé, "Opinions et attitudes des maires ruraux" (unpublished Mémoire, Institut d'Etudes Politiques de Paris, 1964), p. 59. Michel Crozier has noted the contrast in France between a widespread demand for equality and an equally widespread attempt to secure privilege. (Crozier, *The Bureaucratic Phenomenon* [Chicago: University of Chicago Press, 1964], p. 224.)

the national government. In early 1962 Raymond Triboulet, at that time a minister in the Pompidou government and a general councilor from the Calvados, had journeyed to Caen from Paris in order to attend a meeting of the Calvados General Council. M. Triboulet told his colleagues about his strenuous efforts on behalf of the Calvados General Council to obtain a government grant-in-aid for social assistance to residents of the department. M. Triboulet boasted that the national government had never before given a grant to a general council for this purpose. He modestly assumed only part of the credit for obtaining the grant; unfortunately, he could not guarantee that it would be renewed the following year. In order to secure renewal of the grant, he said:

I don't want to conceal the fact that there is a long battle ahead of us. . . . It is a difficult task and will require, I believe, the cooperation of every one of us, of our legislators [senators and deputies from the Calvados], and of myself; of course, I will do all I possibly can, but we can't be completely sure the cause is won.[2]

A former cabinet minister asserts that "the legislator is *first and above all* an elected representative: vis-à-vis the national government, he is the lawyer who protects the general interests of his constituency and the special interests of the families that live there."[3]

Legislators maintain that their efforts are crucial to the success of a commune's application. A deputy stressed the importance of casework, "There are many communes in France. Unless you take personal charge of the dossiers, they get lost in the ministries. You have to see them through."

Senators, in particular, assert that their chief duty is to

2 Raymond Triboulet, before the General Council of the Calvados; reported in the *Délibérations du conseil* (Caen: Préfecture de Calvados, January–February 1962), p. 124.
3 Robert Buron, *Le Plus beau des métiers* (Paris: Plon, 1963), p. 22. (Italics in original.) A significant proportion of French legislators' mail is from mayors writing in regard to local projects. See Marie-Therèse Lancelot, "Le Courrier d'un parlementaire," *Revue française de science politique*, XII (June 1962), 426–32.

represent the communes and the mayors of their constituency. One senator smiled, when asked whether his work for constituents was effective. "Well, you know," he said, "the nearer you are to the stove, the warmer you get." Another senator said, "Mayors choose us to be their lawyer."[4] And a third senator elaborated, "Mayors are organized into a kind of trade union led by their senators."

Nonetheless, a certain tension prevails between a mayor and his legislative representatives. Despite their most earnest efforts, deputies and senators cannot efface the years spent in Paris. They may affect a rustic manner of dress, slip back into the *patois*, and criticize the "technocrats" who make arbitrary decisions in a Paris ministry. Yet legislators' origins may be regarded as less important than their present position: they themselves are very much part of the state. The difficulty is compounded by the possibility that soliciting a legislator's help may antagonize state officials, whose support is essential.[5]

The typical way legislators render a mayor assistance is to perform a *démarche*, a process similar to casework in the United States in which legislators try to influence the national government.[6] The deputy writes to the *cabinet* (personal staff) of the minister or prefect, in order to endorse a project. The purpose of his letter is to expedite the requisite state authorization for the commune's project and, if the project in question is in the category of those subsidized by the national government, to obtain a grant-in-aid for the commune.

Do legislators' efforts have the desired effect? Can legisla-

[4] The senator referred to the fact that senators are elected by a departmental electoral college which is mostly composed of mayors and municipal councilors. For the organized efforts of legislator mayors on behalf of local governments, see Charles Roig, "L'Administration locale et les changements sociaux," in Institut d'Etudes Politiques de Grenoble (ed.), *Administration traditionnelle et planification régionale* (Paris: Armand Colin, 1964), pp. 15–16.

[5] Jean-Pierre Worms has called attention to the struggle between the prefect and political parties to represent local leaders. (Worms, "Le Préfet et ses notables," *Sociologie du travail*, VIII [July–September 1966], 271.)

[6] For the casework of legislators, see Buron, *op. cit.*, pp. 22–34.

tive casework change a decision on a dossier from unfavorable to favorable? Can casework hasten the government's necessary legal approval and financial support? Or does casework have no influence at all on bureaucratic decisions?

Curiously, mayors themselves appear not to be concerned with these questions. They have faith in the "necessary" procedures to follow in order to obtain government support. Most mayors believe that, if they can interest a legislator in their project, it will inevitably redound to their advantage. Charles d'Aragon observes, "*Démarches* aren't always necessary, but they are always considered to be."[7]

Does a mayor's political party influence which legislator he asks for assistance? French political parties appeal to limited and stable segments of the population; there appears to be relatively little transfer of votes from one established party to another.[8] It has been argued that influence flows in "vertical" channels in France: one stays within one's own political and ideological sector and has little to do with those who are not party colleagues.[9] Under these circumstances, one might predict that a mayor would seek help from legislators of his own rather than of another political party and that party crossover for casework would be rare. If mayors sought help from legislators who belonged to rival parties, one might expect legislators to refuse.

In interviews, however, legislators said that they welcomed

[7] Charles d'Aragon, "Le Village et les pouvoirs," in Jacques Fauvet and Henri Mendras (eds.), *Les Paysans et la politique* (Paris: Armand Colin, 1958), p. 508. The question will be examined later in this chapter and in Chapter VI. Some evidence suggests that legislators may prove helpful in obtaining government support.

[8] Georges Dupeux, "Le Comportement des électeurs français de 1958 à 1962," in François Goguel (ed.), *Le Référendum d'octobre et les élections de novembre 1962* (Paris: Armand Colin, 1965), pp. 181–82. François Goguel has argued that even the apparently surprising results of the 1965 presidential elections were consistent with traditional voting patterns. (Goguel, "L'Election présidentielle française de décembre 1965," *Revue française de science politique*, XVI [April 1966], 221–54.)

[9] For evidence corrobating these hypotheses, see Duncan MacRae, Jr., *Parliament, Parties, and Society in France, 1946–1958* (New York: St. Martin's Press, 1967), Chaps. 2, 8–10.

a mayor's demands regardless of his partisan affiliation. One senator maintained that he and his colleagues would perform favors for any mayor who asked. "In fact," he said, laughing, "I prefer someone from another party to seek my help—for he can be won over that way. It's like that in the United States too, isn't it?" A Socialist deputy expressed the same opinion. While Socialist mayors outside his district sought his help, non-Socialist mayors in his district also addressed requests to him and, "I devote as much care to these requests as to requests from my political allies." In one canton, represented by a Socialist deputy, "the fact that he was strongly identified with the left was of no importance to rightist mayors."[1]

In an article on "the new deputy," Pierre Viansson-Ponté observes that, in many constituencies, "candidates will be elected who appear most capable of extracting funds and protection from the Providential State—without ideological considerations or even local attachments playing a part."[2]

The author of a study of rural mayors confesses:

What struck me most is that the political affiliation of the deputy whom mayors ask for help is unimportant. Mayors seek a deputy who is influential. By comparison, a legislator's partisan affiliation or personal qualities are relatively unimportant.[3]

Mayors of opposition parties might address requests to a UNR deputy. One mayor said that Jacques Chaban-Delmas, mayor of Bordeaux and president of the National Assembly, had been extremely helpful to him in obtaining government approval for an industrial zone. The mayor had received

[1] Hélie de Noailles, "Le Maire face aux problèmes communaux dans la région parisienne" (unpublished Mémoire, Institut d'Etudes Politiques de Paris, 1964), p. 50.
[2] Pierre Viansson-Ponté, "Le Nouveau député," *Le Monde*, July 8, 1966. For evidence that in recent years there has been a rise in the proportion of *parachutistes*—deputies elected from constituencies in which they had not formerly resided, see Mattei Dogan, "Le Personnel politique et la personnalité charismatique," *Revue française de sociologie*, VI (July–September 1965), 305–24.
[3] Eric Degremont, "Les Maires ruraux, leur autorité" (unpublished Mémoire, Institut d'Etudes Politiques de Paris, 1965), pp. 77–78.

Chaban-Delmas' help despite the fact that the two men belonged to different political parties and that the mayor was not in Chaban-Delmas' electoral district.

Cooperation across party lines does not, therefore, appear to be uncommon. One former deputy told how he continued to maintain friendly relations with the deputy who had defeated him for re-election. The incumbent deputy had even asked his defeated rival to contact a ministry on behalf of communes in the district. When asked why he had agreed, he replied, "Well, the deputies from the Gironde are pretty friendly, regardless of party." This represents an extreme case of what Jacques Fauvet observes, "Deputies who belong to the same profession or the same part of the country often get on better with each other than with their fellow party members."[4]

A Communist deputy related that he held office hours in a café once a week at which time anyone was welcome to present requests. Non-Communist mayors asked his help, as did constituents who were not members of the working class. Several mayors in a canton represented by a Communist general councilor find it difficult to collaborate with him on local projects; yet other mayors "feel obligated to ignore their differences of opinion [with the general councilor] in order to serve better the interests of the population both represent."[5]

Christian Prieur reports that a "Communist mayor devoted to his rural commune customarily writes to an Independent when he needs a deputy's help; their collaboration is completely non-partisan."[6] Robert Buron notes that "Socialist and even Communist deputies are among the best protectors of the capitalist enterprises in their constituency."[7]

[4] Jacques Fauvet, *The Cockpit of France* (London: Harvill, 1960), p. 124.
[5] De Noailles, *op. cit.*, p. 42.
[6] Christian Prieur, "La Campagne électorale dans l'Aveyron," in Maurice Duverger, François Goguel, and Jean Touchard (eds.), *Les Elections du 2 janvier 1956* (Paris: Armand Colin, 1957), pp. 331–32.
[7] Buron, *op. cit.*, p. 22.

The nature of a project often influences the choice of a legislator. A mayor general councilor related:

You have to ask the politicians for help. . . . One selects them not because of their party affiliation, but because of their usefulness. [Georges] Bonnet [deputy from Dordogne], former Minister of Finance [in the Third Republic], still has friends and prestige at the ministry. It's the same for Robert Lacoste [another deputy from Dordogne], former Minister of Production.[8]

A mayor is eager to find legislators familiar with the type of project he is sponsoring, preferably legislators who have influence in the ministry that distributes the grant for a mayor's proposed project. One mayor reported that he had quickly secured a government grant for a new school, thanks to the help of a senator who sat on the Senate Education Commission. Another mayor said that an application for a regional hospital had been expedited by a deputy who sat on the National Assembly Commission for Health.[9]

A senator from the Gironde stated that the senators of the department were informally specialized to process mayors' requests. One senator was especially valuable: a member of

[8] De Beaucé interviews.

[9] The following anecdote, which Christian Prieur relates, *op. cit.*, p. 331, illustrates the possible value of a deputy's help: "The support of a legislator can be decisive. On the plateau of Montbazens-Rignac there was a group of communes which, because the region was arid, were without a system of public water supply. An intercommunal association was formed twenty years ago [to construct a common system of water supply]. The project was studied but proved premature. There was hesitation, and the financing proved difficult. Eventually, a deputy became interested in the problem and took the question to heart. He knew on which doors to knock and which grants were available. He exerted influence on government bureaus and a year later the pipelines were ready to be installed. Forty-five communes will have water in several months." Buron, *op. cit.*, p. 26, also describes how a deputy tries to hasten a favorable decision by the Rural Engineers Corps on a municipal water system and tries to secure a grant for the commune from the Ministry of the Interior. The *cumul* of municipal and parliamentary office is criticized by Michel Debré, *La République et son pouvoir* (Paris: Nagel, 1950), pp. 171–72, because of the advantage it gives a legislator mayor in dealing with government administrators.

the Senate Finance Commission, he could help mayors on local tax matters.

While party crossover is common when mayors seek legislators' support, a mayor who shares party affiliation with a given legislator feels that he deserves particular consideration from him. Mayors are bitter toward their representative when common party membership has not brought additional benefits. One mayor related that he and his deputy belonged to the same party and, although he had worked in the deputy's behalf during the previous election campaign, the deputy had not been attentive enough to his subsequent requests for help. As a consequence, the mayor had decided to oppose the deputy's renomination.

At a departmental meeting of the Radical Socialist Party, a Radical mayor complained that the deputy in his district did not treat him with due courtesy. The Radicals had formed a coalition with several parties in the Gironde (the Entente Démocratique), and the winning candidate, although an Independent, had been the beneficiary of the Radical mayor's support. However, the mayor now felt that the deputy had not sufficiently reciprocated his support. Thus, while mayors feel that partisan affiliation should be regarded as important when it is beneficial, they themselves do not hesitate crossing party lines in order to seek help from representatives of other parties.

Legislators naturally try to foster the appearance of being powerful. In one department the prefecture informs general councilors when their constituents' applications for loans from a departmental fund have been approved. The councilor, in turn, notifies the recipients in his canton—thereby implying that the recipient's success was due to the general councilor's efforts.[1]

[1] Worms interviews. A similar procedure is common in the United States: when the government makes awards to individuals or communities, the local congressman is usually the first to contact the recipient with the good news.

One administrator reported that legislators occasionally make requests that simply cannot be met. However, "the refusal doesn't endanger our relations. The legislator knows he will be refused, but he needs a little something to show his constituents why it is impossible to meet their request."[2]

When asked about the value of his legislator, one mayor provided indirect corroboration of this process: "They're no help. They go through all the motions but the only concrete result is an elegant letter—nothing more."

Another mayor agreed that deputies and senators were not especially influential in getting applications expedited. He felt that it was better to make inquiries oneself. Pointing to the *Bottin administratif*—which lists the names and telephone numbers of men who occupy administrative positions—he said, "If you know the name of the person you're calling, you get much better results. And if they know it's the mayor of the commune calling, they're more likely to help you. Most mayors rely on others too much and don't use their own initiative."

A Socialist deputy proudly told how he had been decisive in securing government approval for an industrial park in a neighboring commune. He said, "I'm ready to help all those who want me to, but I'm particularly happy to start near home." However, the mayor in whose commune the park was located ascribed his success in gaining government approval for the park to Chaban-Delmas' influence.[3] When the mayor was asked if he had sought the Socialist deputy's help, he replied, "Oh yes. He's my deputy so I thought I'd better see him too. But I don't think he had much to do with it."[4]

---

[2] *Ibid.*
[3] The mayor belonged neither to the UNR nor the Socialist Party.
[4] Laurence Wylie relates that Marseilles' Radical Socialist newspaper gave Edouard Daladier credit for obtaining a grant for a school in Peyrane, while Marseilles' Socialist newspaper attributed the commune's good fortune to the Socialist Minister of Education. (Wylie, *Village in the Vaucluse* [New York: Harper & Row, 1964], pp. 223–27.)

Government administrators assert that legislators' attempts to influence the bureaucracy are generally unsuccessful. A division chief in the Ministry of the Interior stated that specified procedures were followed in processing any commune's application.[5] Stipulated criteria governed the order in which communes were given grants.[6] A bureau chief, responsible for distributing local grants, denied that efforts by deputies were influential. The only circumstances under which a legislator's effort might expedite a commune's application was when the application had not been completed properly or necessary documents had been omitted. By inquiring about the status of a commune's application, a deputy could learn of such an irregularity before the commune was informed and thereby help the commune to rectify the oversight within a short time.

An official in the Ministry of Tourism did not believe that informal influence was generally necessary in order to secure a government grant. He felt that any commune legally eligible could probably obtain a grant if only it were willing to wait. He cited the example of winter sports facilities, with which he was currently concerned. The sudden growth of interest in winter sports had led the government to make grants available for skiing stations and other winter sports facilities. The communes that had applied were allotted grants—on the basis of seniority and often quite unwisely—although many of the communes applying were without influential patrons.

Officials in the Ministry of the Interior admitted that some government funds were devoted to purely partisan ends. The

---

[5] Evidence here and below is from interviews conducted with officials of the Direction Générale des Collectivités Locales, Ministry of the Interior, Paris, in the Winter 1963.

[6] However, until recently, ministries and even divisions within ministries had great freedom to determine the rules by which grants shall be given. According to officials in the Ministry of the Interior, the single most important factor was usually seniority of application. In order to minimize controversy, priority was mostly given in the order in which applications arrived at the ministry. While in recent years national and regional planning have changed the procedures for allocating government grants, the result has been to reduce even further the efficacy of legislators' casework.

minister had a small sum—a *reliquat* (remainder) that was available after other expenses were met—which he could distribute as grants for local improvements to whichever commune he chose. Moreover, the government has occasionally hinted that it would make an exceptional effort for its friends. During the 1965 municipal election campaign, Prime Minister Pompidou implied that communes who followed the spirit of the Fifth Republic by voting UNR in the forthcoming elections would be given special help "to progress at the same rhythm as the state."[7] It was such statements that prompted François Mitterrand to charge that French local governments:

. . . *increasingly find their freedoms infringed upon by the national government. Municipalities, particularly those that voted the 'wrong way,' are arbitrarily deprived of the resources they are legally allowed and which they need for their development.*[8]

However, while a definitive judgment is impossible, it appears that political favoritism is extremely rare and that most grants are given without regard to partisan considerations. At the least, one might question whether legislators' efforts on behalf of mayors are as influential as legislators assert. Mayors assume that the state is basically unwilling to approve and subsidize local projects. A mayor suspects that, when the state wants him to undertake a project, the project will benefit the "they" rather than the commune.[9] And he assumes that, when *he* requests assistance for a project from the state, the only way it can be obtained is by skillful manipulation.

Mayors do not try to reconcile their firmly held belief that the state is an adversary with the plainly observable fact that the state actually encourages local improvements. The legislator's support, therefore, becomes especially important. He

[7] *Le Monde*, March 11, 1965.
[8] François Mitterrand, "France is no Longer a Democracy," *The New York Times Magazine*, May 29, 1966, p. 56.
[9] Laurence Wylie, *op. cit.*, Chap. 10.

is needed to act as intermediary with the hostile power because, presumably, he possesses occult information that will expedite the affair. Legislators attempt to exaggerate the influence they actually have in order to maximize constituent support.

Mayors follow an intricate procedure when they undertake local projects. One step of the procedure is to secure active support within the commune, particularly from the municipal council. Another step is to enlist the support of their legislators, even when it may not be necessary. Mayors are careful to seek legislators' support; legislators, themselves, are pleased to be asked. Party factors do not appear to influence either the mayor's selection of a legislator or the legislator's response. The ostensible reason for such elaborate precautions is to prepare for the confrontation with the state. Mayors direct particular effort toward obtaining approval from subordinate government officials in the administrative hierarchy.

Chapter VI

State Approval of Local Projects

Once a mayor decides to undertake an important project, he needs to obtain the legal approval and the financial support of the national government. Despite their fierce desire for local autonomy, therefore, local officials are closely dependent on the national government. A local officeholder feels forced to cultivate good relations with national officials although he is suspicious of their intentions. Since he assumes the state to be hostile to communal wishes, the mayor believes he must placate the government administrators who might affect the success of his venture.

The suspicions of local officeholders are not unfounded. National officials are often critical of local incompetence. The government would prefer having greater freedom in local matters and would prefer not having to seek the cooperation of local officials.

According to one mayor, " 'Madame de' [the state] is a flirt, an enormous flirt, and in order to obtain more from her than mere promises, she must be courted assiduously and shown proof of a loyalty without blemish."[1] A rural mayor

[1] J.-L. Quereillahc, *Un tel . . . maire* (Paris: Editions France-Empire, 1962), p. 99.

lavishly praises his subprefect's help: "It is beyond question that without the early and persistent efforts of M. *le Sous-préfet*, our project [for a new school] would still be in the planning stage."[2] Another mayor remarks wistfully, after his subprefect has done him a favor, "Doesn't it prove that when . . . a subprefect takes a project seriously in hand, many things are possible?"[3]

The French mayor has evolved a cautious strategy for dealing with his prefect and subprefect. One of the two must approve the municipal council deliberation initiating a project, and the mayor fears that this approval may not be forthcoming without his first carefully laying the groundwork. Upon being asked about his relations with the prefecture, one mayor replied, "Yes, I get along well. But that's no accident. You have to study the terrain carefully." The mayor's preparations are rather taxing: before the municipal council formally passes a deliberation, the mayor not only visits his influential municipal councilors, but also takes the precaution of contacting officials in the prefecture. They may suggest ways in which a project should be modified in order for it to become acceptable to the prefecture. A prefect's chief aide (*chef de cabinet*) admitted: "The friendship of a division chief may facilitate the preparation of a project. His cooperation [with the mayor] may help to make the project acceptable to the prefect."[4]

Such negotiation between mayor and prefecture borders on the illegal, for French administrative law actually forbids the "tutelary authority" (see Appendix B) to modify municipal council deliberations. A deliberation must be either approved or disapproved in its entirety by the prefect or subprefect. The revision of municipal council deliberations, however, is a wide-

[2] Pierre Wantzenriether, "Le Maire rural et son sous-préfet," *Etude des problèmes municipaux*, no. 6 (June 1965), p. 27.
[3] Ernest Monpied, *Terres mouvantes, un maire rural au coeur du remembrement* (Paris: Les Editions Ouvrières, 1965), p. 14.
[4] De Beaucé interviews.

spread practice, and is desired by both mayor and prefecture.[5]

While preliminary negotiations are being conducted with the prefecture, a mayor also contacts officials in the specialized ministries. Aside from his need for technical assistance from them, he seeks to nullify potential opposition as early as possible. A wise mayor takes no chances of alienating a ministry. Rather than run the risk of offending an official, he chooses the prudent course and maximizes the number of ministries whom he informally consults on a project.

Quereillahc's "typical" mayor expresses a fear common among mayors, when he talks of the "war among the [technical] services. . . . Sometimes a single grain of sand can throw an otherwise perfectly functioning machine completely out of control."[6] The mayor in the novel succeeds in soothing the ruffled feelings of the departmental planning official by inviting him to an important meeting of mayors.

One mayor said during an interview that the subprefect of his *arrondissement* was always invited when mayors of the canton had a meeting. The invitation was actually extended in the hope of gaining the subprefect's support for local projects; it was both a form of flattery and a way in which mayors could communicate their demands directly.[7]

A mayor thus confers with prefectural and technical officials in order to obtain assurance for the approval of his project; this informal consultation precedes the initial munici-

[5] Hervé Detton, "L'Administration et la vie locale" (mimeographed course notes, Institut d'Etudes Politiques de Paris, 1961–62); Roland Maspétiol and Pierre Laroque, *La Tutelle administrative* (Paris: Sirey, 1930), p. 326; and Charles Schmitt, *Le Maire de la commune rurale* (Paris: Berger-Levrault, 1959), Chap. 6.

[6] Quereillahc, *op. cit.*, p. 125. But the mayor also suggests that technical officials can be of real assistance to mayors (*ibid.*, p. 173).

[7] Quereillahc relates a similar process in which the local prefect attends a meeting of mayors who review the conscription list. After the meeting the prefect receives requests from the assembled mayors. (*Ibid.*, pp. 109–19.) On presidential tours in the provinces, General de Gaulle met mayors in a similar fashion. André Passeron, *De Gaulle parle* (Paris: Plon, 1962), pp. 546–47.

pal council deliberation. The purpose of "preclearance" is, of course, to forestall potential roadblocks before a dossier is formally launched. Thus, the prefectural officials who advise the mayor initially about a project are later required by law to pass judgment on that same project. And they use as evidence in forming their judgment the opinions of technical ministry officials who have also participated in the informal stages of planning a project.

Not all proposals that are informally negotiated with the prefecture even need to be formally submitted to the state for a review of their desirability. Some proposals fall into the category of those that are merely submitted to a review of their legality. However, one municipal councilor naively, but understandably, confused law with fact when he discussed the question of why all projects were informally negotiated beforehand with the prefecture: "The commune is under the 'tutelage' of the state and it can't do a thing without consulting the services [of the prefecture]. Otherwise it won't get any grants-in-aid." The result—forbidden by law—is that "the bureaus of the prefecture tell us whether a project will be approved before it's voted."

A mayor voluntarily bargains with state officials and accepts their advice because he fears that unless state approval is sought early, the state may later retaliate by withholding vital financial support.

Brian Chapman rightly notes that "the prefect's task on these occasions is very delicate and fraught with political difficulties, and tutelage involves questions of policy and finesse that are often overlooked by writers on the subject."[8] One might add that the mayor's task is equally delicate and fraught with political difficulties. Each of the participants in the drama feels that his role must be played with the utmost skill if the play is to end successfully. Because the actors feel

[8] Brian Chapman, An Introduction to French Local Government (London: George Allen & Unwin, 1953), p. 57.

the outcome of the drama to be so important, the drama itself becomes invested with danger. Mayors feel that great care must be taken to foresee all possible pitfalls.

During the course of an interview, mayors would evaluate the prefecture in two contradictory ways. On the one hand, a mayor would boast of his cordial relations with officials of the prefecture. He would relate how he could reach the prefect on the telephone whenever he wanted and how he gained prefectural approval for his proposals. In brief, he appeared quite satisfied with existing arrangements. On the other hand, when the more abstract question arose of the general relations between state and commune, the mayor pictured the situation very differently. He would then bitterly decry the state's interference with local autonomy, complaining about the *chinoiserie*—finicky attention to details—that characterized state officials. He would denounce state supervision and angrily deny its necessity.[9]

What is the reason for a mayor's contradictory attitudes? One possible answer might be that when the concrete question of personal relations with state officials is raised, a mayor has an interest in exaggerating the harmony of these relations. He cites this harmony as evidence that he can successfully manipulate the state; furthermore, he enjoys his contact with state officials. Mayors are proud of their acquaintance with important personages and delight in using their wits to outsmart the state.[1] Upon being asked how he liked visiting the prefecture in connection with his duties, one mayor replied:

[9] There are frequent criticisms of administrative centralization in France. See Charles Brindillac, "Décoloniser la France," *Esprit*, XXV (December 1957); Paul Lambin, "Projet de défense de l'autonomie des communes rurales," *Départements et communes* (July–August 1960); and the annual report of the secretary-general of the Association of French Mayors, published each year in *Départements et communes*.

[1] Mayors frequently introduced me to their constituents by saying that the prefect had suggested I visit the commune. Their statement was not less significant for being untrue in most cases. In "Le Préfet et ses notables," *Sociologie du travail*, VIII (July–September 1966), 260–71,

"Very much. That's where I get my greatest pleasure."[2] Yet when the abstract question of relations between the national and local government is raised, the mayor expresses anger at the commune's legal and actual dependence on the state, feeling it to be degrading and hypocritical for him to be forced into maintaining cordial relations with state officials. On the one hand, the mayor is proud of how he can translate the good relations he fosters into communal improvements: the commune benefits from his skillful leadership. On the other hand, he resents being forced to play what he regards as an essentially false game. Since the mayor believes that a conflict of interest necessarily exists between state and commune, how is he to justify his own friendly relations with state officials?

A mayor's situation is rendered still more awkward by his uncertainty about how he is regarded by prefectural officials. Since beneath the outwardly warm feelings that mayors display toward state officials lies the desire to gain certain benefits for the commune, they reason, might not the same thing be true of the feelings state officials have toward them?

A mayor's suspicions on this score are not without foundation. Bureaucrats at one prefecture said that they resented mayors' visits more than those of other citizens. One bureaucrat asserted, "I deplore the negligence and misinformation of small-town mayors."[3] Another related: "I receive them [mayors] often. They are very pleasant and full of good will; they are even touching. But they *cannot* know the problems. They aren't qualified to know them."[4] A bureau chief, in charge of communal affairs, said that he preferred seeing town

---

Jean-Pierre Worms analyzes perceptively the symbiotic relationship between mayors and prefect. Although apparently contradictory, mutual respect between mayors and prefect and even a tacit alliance does not exclude their also opposing each other on some issues.

[2] De Beaucé interviews.
[3] Worms interviews.
[4] *Ibid.* (Italics in original.)

clerks to mayors, who "take themselves too seriously."[5] The secretary-general of a prefecture, writing in a journal for government administrators, asserts that mayors, particularly rural mayors, are so ignorant that the state's tutelage often borders on direct administration. He concludes, "The rural mentality remains closer to that of subject than citizen. . . ."[6] Administrators talked at length about the need for France to remain highly centralized because of the ineptitude of local officials. During an interview, one subprefect made a wry face when he was informed by his secretary that a particular mayor was trying to reach him on the telephone. More generally, the French prefectural corps is traditionally reputed to subscribe to a philosophy of extreme centralization.[7] State officials do not merely adhere to a doctrine of centralization. The state also attempts in practice to assure local conformity with its own policies. By means of pressure and financial inducements, it tries to persuade mayors to undertake local projects and to form intercommunal cooperative arrangements—all of which call forth local hostility. The veiled animosity which is one facet of the relationship between mayors and state officials makes more understandable the intricate strategy that mayors

[5] *Ibid*. Morton Grodzins observed a similar pattern in the relations of American local officials with national officials. He suggested that professional or technical officials share a common outlook, regardless of whether they work for the state or national government, whereas political officials from different levels of government are more disposed to conflict. See also Morton Grodzins, "Centralization and Decentralization in the American Federal System," in Robert A. Goldwin (ed.), *A Nation of States* (Chicago: Rand McNally & Co., 1963).

[6] Jean Brenas, "La Fonction préfectorale," *Bulletin d'information de l'association du corps préfectoral* . . . (September 1959), p. 27.

[7] See, for further examples, the *Mémoires de Stage* written by students at the Ecole Nationale d'Administration—the elite school for future government administrators—which uniformly recommend further centralization: Pierre Bandet, "L'Avenir des petites communes de la Manche" (unpublished Mémoire, Ecole Nationale d'Administration, 1958); Hubert Husson, "L'Avenir des petites communes" (unpublished Mémoire, Ecole Nationale d'Administration, 1960); and Jacques Magnet, "Les Petites communes en Charente" (unpublished Mémoire, Ecole Nationale d'Administration, 1960).

follow to obtain help from the state. Yet is the procedure itself responsible in the event of success?

Just how important is adherence to the protocol that most mayors feel obliged to observe? Is it, in fact, necessary to enlist the assistance of political representatives? Will bureau and division chiefs at the prefecture and in Paris ministries actually sabotage projects from mayors who do not follow the customary informal procedure? Mayors believe that unless they follow the prescribed ritual they may fail to receive the help they want from the state. Legislators assert that without their delicate maneuvering the state would delay or reject a commune's application. Yet state officials argue, contrary to both, that they are perfectly willing to grant financial assistance to communes for local projects. Rather than having to be pressured or manipulated to grant benefits, state officials relate how they encourage mayors to undertake communal improvements.

One group of mayors generally does not follow the customary procedure. The mayors in this group do not cultivate strategically placed state officials and are, in fact, their political enemies. Often they do not even request help from their deputy and senator when applying for government grants. Yet such mayors are remarkably active: they apply for and receive numerous government grants; they undertake a variety of public projects, and their communes support numerous public facilities. Communist mayors have a keen sense of the possibilities open to their communes and they undertake ambitious programs of local improvements. They are reputed to be among the most conscientious and competent mayors in France.

Communist mayors have earned the grudging respect of many government officials. Although bureaucrats are not eager to help Communists consolidate their local positions by supplying them with grants-in-aid, Communist mayors complete their applications for grants in the proper fashion and otherwise follow the stipulated procedures.[8] They are both capable and persistent and, as a result, probably receive more state aid than any comparable group of French mayors.[9]

State officials, as well as both Communist and non-Communist mayors, agree that Communist mayors have relatively little difficulty getting applications for grants approved.[1] As one highly placed bureaucrat said, "If I lived in a rural commune, I'd vote Communist even though I'm against the party. Communist mayors get more done for their communes than any other mayors I know."

[8] A study of mayors in a canton of the Seine-et-Oise found that the one Communist mayor of the canton knew the technical aspect of a mayor's position better than did any other mayor in the canton. Hélie de Noailles, "Le Maire face aux problèmes communaux dans la région parisienne" (unpublished Mémoire, Institut d'Etudes Politiques de Paris, 1964), p. 18. According to Philip M. Williams, "The Communists were successful municipally because they were efficient and capable administrators." (Williams, Crisis and Compromise, 3rd ed. [Hamden, Conn.: Shoe String Press, 1964], p. 331.) See also Antoine Olivesi and Marcel Roncayolo, Géographie électorale des Bouches-du-Rhône sous la IVᵉ République (Paris: Armand Colin, 1961), p. 133. In recent years, Jaciste (young progressive Catholic) mayors have also proved dynamic and effective.

[9] There are no statistics available of total government grants from all ministries to each commune. The judgment is based on interviews with national officials and Communist mayors. However, even Communist mayors may follow the "orthodox" procedure described in this chapter. See the example related by Christian Prieur, "La Campagne électorale dans l'Aveyron," in Maurice Duverger, François Goguel, and Jean Touchard (eds.), Les Elections du 2 janvier 1956 (Paris: Armand Colin, 1957), pp. 331-32.

[1] Charles Roig quotes extreme left mayors who say they have good relations with departmental administrators. (Roig, "L'Administration locale et les changements sociaux," in Institut d'Etudes Politiques de Grenoble [ed.], Administration traditionnelle et planification régionale ([Paris: Armand Colin, 1964], p. 48.) A political commentator went so far as to ascribe the rise in Communist voting strength in the 1959 local elections, as compared with the 1958 legislative elections, "to the activity and competence of its municipal officeholders. . . ." (A. Delcroix, "L'Echec de l'U.N.R., est-il celui de de Gaulle?" France Observateur [March 12, 1959], pp. 3-4.) Gordon Wright tells how a Communist mayor tried to satisfy all requests for help, even if they came from those living outside the commune. For example, he describes how the mayor used great effort to ensure that his commune had . . . a priest! "Mayor Jean's convictions did not stand in the way of his duty. . . ." (Wright, Rural Revolution in France [Stanford, Calif.: Stanford University Press, 1964], p. 196.)

The success of Communist mayors suggests that adherence to the informal protocol may not be necessary in order to secure state benefits. Yet why, then, do most mayors misunderstand government intentions? What sustains their apparently false belief in the necessity for the informal ritual?

Mayoral behavior becomes more explicable in the light of the local unity that mayors are anxious to preserve. If state grants are in fact as difficult to obtain as mayors say, local disagreements would weaken a commune's chances of obtaining grants. The presumed difficulty in obtaining state support thus helps enforce communal solidarity. To achieve this solidarity the mayor cites his arduous efforts as evidence that the state is a formidable opponent. Conflict with the state makes even more apparent the need for communal solidarity: there is a benefit to be gained from following the informal procedure even when it is not needed for achieving the ostensible goal.

And yet the clash between state and commune transcends specific controversies.

Chapter VII

Opposition Between State and Commune

Partisan differences exacerbate the inherent suspicion French mayors feel toward the state. In the 1960's the state meant the Gaullist state, to which most mayors were firmly opposed. The percentage of UNR mayors in France was extremely low, despite the fact that there had been two general municipal elections during the Fifth Republic. Most mayors of this period belonged to political parties that opposed the UNR; they were initially elected to office before General de Gaulle regained power, and were re-elected in 1959 and 1965. A comparison of the political party affiliation of municipal councilors elected in the 1959 and 1965 municipal elections with that of deputies elected in the 1958, 1962, and 1967 legislative elections (Table 7) shows a striking disparity in UNR strength.

Whereas 41 per cent of the deputies elected in the legislative elections of 1967 were affiliated with the UNR, only 9 per cent of the municipal councilors elected in 1965 identified themselves as members of the Gaullist party. General de Gaulle had repeatedly criticized "the men and parties of former times."[1] In an interview prior to the 1965 municipal

---

[1] Address by President Charles de Gaulle, November 7, 1962.

Table 7
Municipal Councilors and Deputies; Distribution by Party
(rounded to nearest whole per cent)

PARTY	MUNICIPAL COUNCILORS		DEPUTIES		
	1959	1965	1958	1962	1967
Communist	4%	4%	2%	9%	15%
Non-Communist left	6	3	0	0	1
Socialist	11	9	9	14 ⎫	
Radical[a]	21	19	6	9 ⎬	25
UNR	5	9	41	49	41
MRP	7	5	13	8	9
Moderates[b]	36	9	29	10	9
Local Party	9	44	0	0	0

[a] The table combines the rubrics used by the Ministry of the Interior for Radicals, and Center and Center Left.
[b] The right has undergone numerous changes since 1958. The one category combines several divergent positions. Moreover, on the local level, the distinction between Moderates and Local Party is not sharp; this explains the seemingly great shift in the strength of the two groups between 1959 and 1965.
SOURCE: L'Année politique, 1958, pp. 45–46; ibid., 1959, p. 33; ibid., 1962, p. 127; ibid., 1965, p. 25; and Le Monde, April 5, 1967.

elections, Prime Minister Pompidou exhorted voters "to eliminate the *régime des partis* from all levels of public life."[2]

Specific policies of the government increased mayoral opposition, for example, the government's attempts to deal with the plethora of small communes in France. Government decrees of January 1959 created two new forms of intercommunal groupings—one for urban areas, the other for rural communes—to deal with the problem.[3] Prior to the January

[2] *Le Monde*, March 11, 1965.
[3] One, the urban district (*district urbain*), grouped a large city and the surrounding communes. The second permitted communes to administer several services in common; it was called the Intercommunal Association for Multiple Purposes (*Syndicat de Commune à Vocation Multiple*)—

1959 reform, membership in an intercommunal association was voluntary: an intercommunal association could be created only with the consent of every commune within the proposed grouping.

Table 8

Purposes for Which the Intercommunal
Associations Were Created

PURPOSE	NUMBER
Water Supply	2,768
Electrification	1,697
Road Construction and Repair	459
Agriculture: Drainage, Flood Prevention, etc.	469
Education: Upkeep of Schools, Transportation, etc.	396
Construction Projects	115
Sewage Disposal	133
Miscellaneous	378
	6,415

SOURCE: Unpublished figures, supplied by the Service de l'Action Economique, Ministry of the Interior, January 1964.

Under the provisions of the two new intercommunal groupings, the national government might force a commune to join, despite the opposition of its municipal council.[4] If

French Government Regulations 59.29 and 59.30, January 5, 1959. See also Jean-Jacques Delarce, "Réforme territoriale des communes" (unpublished Mémoire, Institut d'Etudes Politiques de Paris, 1962); Jacques Roy, "L'Administration intercommunale" (unpublished thesis, University of Bordeaux, Faculty of Law, 1944); Louis-Georges Verdun, *Le Groupement des communes en France* (Bordeaux: Bière, 1963); Jacques Trorial and Hubert Astier, "Où en sont les regroupements de communes," *Le Moniteur des travaux publics et du bâtiment*, LXI, no. 3 (April 9, 1966), 17–34; and Jacques Trorial and Hubert Penot, "Urbanisme et structures administratives locales," *Urbanisme*, XXXV (1966), 18–21.

[4] If the majority of the municipal councils with more than two-thirds of the total population of the proposed grouping approved the intercommunal syndicate, the other communes were required to join. If two-thirds of the municipal councils from communes with a majority of the total population approved the syndicate, the other communes were also obliged

the conditions for forming a joint association were met, the Minister of the Interior was authorized to initiate the new grouping. Thus recalcitrant communes were forced to join, to pay taxes to the grouping, and to abide by the decisions taken by the governing board of the association.

Behind mayors' opposition to the intercommunal associations lurked an even greater fear. In the words of one mayor, "The government doesn't want to be bothered by us [mayors]. It's planning to force communes together." The government issued frequent denials that it was contemplating the abolition of small communes.[5] Yet mayors were not reassured.[6] They repeatedly asserted that the government was only waiting for a propitious moment to make a drastic change in the communal structure.[7]

The most drastic confrontation between mayors and the government occurred in March 1963 at the annual convention

---

to join. A further reform, contained in the government's *projet de loi* no. 1946 in 1966, proposed the creation of urban communities in large metropolitan centers. New metropolitan councils would administer functions like housing, urban planning, education, and fire prevention, on a metropolitan-wide basis.

[5] See, for example, remarks by Premier Georges Pompidou in answer to a question by Gaston Defferre, in the National Assembly, *Journal Officiel, Débats Parlementaires*, December 13, 1962, p. 63.

[6] The recommendations of students in the Ecole Nationale d'Administration are unanimously in favor of reducing the number of French communes. See their Mémoires de Stage cited in Chapter VI, Footnote 7, p. 97. More significantly, high government officials privately admitted that the government was determined not to permit the continued existence of what it regarded as an outdated system of local government. If voluntary regrouping of communes did not take place, and the government had sufficient political strength, it planned to carry out fundamental reforms of local government. Criticism of the structure of French local government is not confined to government officials. See Jacques Fauvet's suggestions for reform, *Le Monde*, January 23, 1963.

[7] Other examples of conflict between local officeholders and the national government included proposed reforms of the local tax structure and the 1962 change in the method of electing the President of the Republic. In the latter change, mayors' powers were diminished when the electoral college, which had formerly elected the President—and on which all mayors sat—was abolished in favor of direct election of the President.

of the Association of French Mayors (Association des Maires de France), which includes about three-quarters of France's 38,000 mayors. This confrontation and subsequent events provide a good illustration of the opposition that exists between the national and local governments in France. The conflict played an important part in shaping mayoral attitudes toward the state and was alluded to repeatedly during interviews the following year.

The Association of Mayors, founded in the early twentieth century, was a powerful and respected organization. Edouard Herriot, premier in the Third Republic, mayor of Lyons and president of the National Assembly, served as president of the association after World War II. The association's aim was to defend the interests of French communes and mayors, particularly vis-à-vis the national government.[8] Ministry of the Interior officials informally asked association representatives for advice and information; leaders of the association were frequent visitors to the ministry. Yet the government had been generally unresponsive to such association proposals as the transferral to the national government of expenses hitherto borne by local governments. In recent years the association had repeatedly demanded assurances from the Minister of the Interior that the national government was not planning to restructure local government. Its doubts had not been laid to rest.

[8] The association was not known for its extremist views. French local government associations, of which the Association of Mayors is by far the largest, were severely criticized by the *Manchester Guardian*, March 2, 1955, because they "do not represent the wishes of the local electors or the interests of local government; they stand for nothing but the defence and promotion of the particular forms of local authority, whose obsolescence has made reform so urgently necessary." (Quoted in J. D. Stewart, *British Pressure Groups* [Oxford: Oxford University Press, 1958], p. 243.) For a discussion of the association, which stresses its conservative orientation, see Charles Roig, "L'Administration locale et les changements sociaux," in Institut d'Etudes Politiques de Grenoble (ed.), *Administration traditionnelle et planification régionale* (Paris: Armand Colin, 1964), pp. 16–19, 24–25.

Traditionally, the keynote address at the association's annual convention was delivered by the Minister of the Interior. In 1963 Minister of the Interior Frey was barely able to deliver his speech because of the persistent heckling from mayors that greeted his appearance. The minister left the convention in a rage and thereupon set out systematically to destroy the association.[9]

He ordered all contacts severed between Ministry of the Interior officials and representatives of the association. The association was deprived of its privileged access to the government and the government hoped its value to mayors would correspondingly be weakened.

In place of the Association of Mayors, which was independent of the government, the Ministry of the Interior created an organization of its own, the Welcome Bureau for Mayors and General Councilors (Bureau d'Accueil des Maires et des Conseillers Généraux). Initially, the bureau was created to welcome mayors who had come to Paris on administrative errands. Its staff made hotel and train reservations for mayors and supplied them with information about the government's administrative structure in Paris, so as to facilitate their work.

The assistant chief of the bureau said that the purpose of the bureau was to gain mayoral support for the government. As a result of the political fight waged by the Association of Mayors, local officeholders had lost confidence in the government. In the words of the assistant bureau chief:

It was necessary to re-establish credit and contact with mayors. The mayors were organized in a political machine [the Association of French Mayors]. Topics discussed at its congress included the force de frappe, communal liberties, and the election of the President of the Republic—all political and not administrative matters.[1]

[9] The account that follows is based on interviews with government officials and participants in the controversy, Winter 1963.
[1] The assistant bureau chief meant that a mayors' organization should not be concerned with current political controversies. However, mayors could

The assistant chief contended that the association was not representative: most mayors were not interested in the association; it was run by a few hundred activists and other mayors had little contact with it.

The effect on the Chicago Democratic machine of a newly created information bureau was not unlike what the Ministry of the Interior hoped would happen to the Association of French Mayors:

Even such a seemingly innocuous reform as the establishment of an information bureau in City Hall has weakened the machine. Helping a constituent to find his way through the maze of local governmental organizations was one of the few favors the ward committeeman had left to give. When constituents found that they could get better service by calling the mayor's information bureau, another tie to the machine was cut. If a new tie took its place, it was to the mayor himself or to the City Hall bureaucracy.[2]

The Welcome Bureau was part of the Ministry of the Interior. The minister appointed as bureau chief a subprefect who was known for his familiarity with the difficulties facing small communes.[3] An effort was made to give the bureau an air of independence, for example, by its physical location, which was in a private office building, several blocks from the Ministry of the Interior.

Unlike most government bureaus, the Welcome Bureau was lavishly appointed, its salons large and elegant. The bureau chief was a friendly man who inspired confidence. With the

---

not help but be concerned with matters of communal liberties. Moreover, mayors were members of the electoral college that had formerly elected the President and were, therefore, directly affected by President de Gaulle's proposal in the fall of 1962 to abolish the electoral college in favor of direct election of the President. Not unexpectedly, they were very heavily against the proposal.

[2] Edward Banfield, *Political Influence* (New York: The Free Press of Glencoe, 1961), p. 256.

[3] The appointee was Charles Schmitt, author of *Le Maire de la commune rurale* (Paris: Berger-Levrault, 1959). M. Schmitt was subsequently appointed to Roger Frey's personal *cabinet* and was named a prefect.

help of his well-stocked liquor cabinet, visitors were soon made to feel very much at ease. The bureau made a decidedly good impression.

The government soon decided that the bureau's responsibilities would have to be expanded and its prestige increased if it were to supplant the Association of Mayors. The name of the bureau was changed to the Information Division for Mayors and General Councilors (Service d'Information des Maires et des Conseillers Généraux). Its position in the administrative structure was upgraded.

The tasks of the division were also expanded. A brochure sent to all mayors included pictures of the offices where mayors would be welcomed and explained the division's purpose. "In addition to the customary assistance they receive from departmental administrators [at the prefecture], local officials who travel to Paris will find in the bureau a supplementary means of administrative information and an introduction to ministries for their projects."[4] The Information Division invited mayors to transmit to it their requests for information and for assistance in obtaining government help, implying that it was in a better position to satisfy requests than was the Association of Mayors, deputies, or senators. When a mayor asked the bureau for help, it made every effort to comply.

The government thus created a new organization for mayors (what might be considered a "company union"), after their own organization opposed the government. The government's actions toward mayors resembled its attempt to discredit intermediate organizations in other areas and was part of a general effort to control the channels of communication between itself and its constituents.[5] Gaullist policy toward mayors was consistent with its general political style.

[4] Brochure published by the Bureau d'Information des Maires, Paris (n.d.).
[5] Stanley Hoffmann, "Paradoxes of the French Political Community," in Hoffmann, *et al.*, *In Search of France* (Cambridge: Harvard University Press, 1963), pp. 99–102.

In addition to creating the Mayors' Information Division, the Ministry of the Interior embarked on a related project to renew contact with mayors and to destroy the independent Association of Mayors.[6] It initiated biweekly meetings in Paris of influential mayors from each region of France. A colloquium (Colloque des Maires) was held for one day.[7] The prefects in the departments that comprised one of France's administrative regions invited the prominent mayors in their departments to attend the meeting. The Minister of the Interior instructed prefects which mayors to invite: "His political preference doesn't matter—if he is dynamic and *réalisateur* (gets things done)—and as long as he isn't an unconditional opponent."[8] (By this last phrase, the minister made it clear that Communist mayors were not welcome at a colloquium.)

For each colloquium several hundred mayors from the region would meet in Paris at the Ministry of the Interior. The mayors were divided by department. Their prefect accompanied them to Paris and presided over the working sessions, which consisted of discussions and speeches by technical experts from the government. The agenda of the conference was decided upon by each prefect after consultation with the mayors who were to attend the colloquium. Typical subjects were the new intercommunal associations, schools, and local finances.

A colloquium concluded with an address by the Minister of the Interior and an informal cocktail hour for the assembled mayors. He sang the praises of their region: its cuisine, its fine scenery, its outstanding citizens. In his discussion of questions about municipal government that had arisen during the

---

[6] The Association of Mayors was not destroyed: in fact, its membership increased. However, M. Frey did not address the association at its conventions the following several years. Mayoral opposition to M. Frey may have been one reason why he was not reappointed Minister of the Interior after the March 1967 legislative elections.

[7] The account that follows is based on attendance at four colloquia in the spring of 1964.

[8] Circular from the Minister of the Interior to prefects, December, 1963.

day, he cited the remarks by some of the most distinguished mayors present. In an effort to assure mayors that no major change in national government policy toward local governments was contemplated, he furnished evidence of how the Gaullist Government had stimulated local development and he stressed the government's continued interest. The minister discussed the Mayors' Division, saying that its creation testified to the concern that the government felt for local officials. He then invited mayors to send their requests to the division and assured them that it would be responsive to their desires.

The government's chief purpose in sponsoring the Mayors' Information Division and the colloquia was to obtain the confidence of France's mayors. Twenty-three colloquia were held during 1963–64, attended by six thousand mayors—the most powerful in France, and a significant proportion of all mayors.[9] Neither the bureau nor the colloquia were outright appeals to support the government. In fact, an effort was made to ignore the political conflict between French mayors and their government. Ministry officials who spoke at a colloquium were instructed to confine their remarks to technical subjects: very rarely did broad or controversial matters arise. There was to be no mention of the Association of Mayors, of the opposition of most mayors to the UNR, or of the mayors' well-known suspicions about the government's policies. The government's major objective—the attempt to obtain mayors' confidence—was to come from a silent demonstration that the two forces shared identical goals.

The minister was the only government official who raised questions of policy. And his aim was to make explicit a point that the government had been quietly reiterating throughout the day: that there was no reason for mayors to distrust and oppose the government.

However, both the Mayors' Division and the colloquia

---

[9] For a discussion of the colloquia, see "Une Année de colloques des maires," *Etude des problèmes municipaux*, no. 8 (December 1965).

failed to achieve what the government hoped they would. Although bureaucrats had been instructed not to raise political points at the colloquia, mayors said that they were not misled: they suspected why the government had gone to such elaborate lengths, and they were determined to resist its blandishments. One mayor said it was obvious that the government had not brought mayors to Paris merely to inform them about technical questions: there were better ways in which this information could be transmitted. Since many topics were covered, each had to be dealt with briefly; as a result, mayors couldn't assimilate all the information, and they didn't even try. "So much has been discussed at the colloquium, our heads are spinning!" Another mayor said that, in his opinion, the explanation for the colloquia was "psychological." He discussed the terrible reception accorded M. Frey at the convention of the Association of Mayors. "That's the real reason for all this," he said laughing, indicating the ornate room and the waiters hurrying around with trays laden with *hors d'oeuvres* and champagne.

Some mayors admitted being flattered by the attention paid them, yet they remained on their guard against precisely what the government hoped to accomplish.[1] Although the colloquia were conceived by the government to reduce mayoral opposition, they failed to accomplish their purpose. Opposition between the French commune and the Gaullist state remains fundamental and seemingly irreconcilable.[2]

[1] Many bureaucrats who addressed the colloquia shared the mayors' negative evaluation. Administrators felt that their technical skills were being used to camouflage the government's political aim. They disliked giving speeches at the working sessions. They did not relish the discussions that followed, nor did they enjoy the informal contact with mayors. A visible sign of the cleavage between mayors and administrators was that at receptions of the colloquia, most mayors congregated on one side of the hall and most bureaucrats on the other.

[2] After reading this section, one highly placed administrator commented, in a private communication, "It seems appropriate to add that a great number of mayors regretted the disturbances at the 1963 convention of the French Association of Mayors. They believed it inelegant and mal-

The curious fact is, however, that the style and outlook of the mayors in their own bailiwick is remarkably similar to the style and outlook of the Gaullist regime. If "communal" were substituted for "national," Laurence Wylie's description of General de Gaulle could apply equally well to many French mayors: "Like a good head of the household, playing favorites with no child—but satisfying no one completely—he seemed to be motivated primarily by a desire to preserve the identity and to work for the welfare of the national family as a whole."[3]

Like a French mayor, General de Gaulle maintains that he is an impartial spokesman for his whole constituency rather than for one part of it. Some selections from his writings will help illustrate the political style that French mayors share with their President.[4] General de Gaulle asserts that the traditional democratic methods of reaching political office through an appeal for support do not apply to him. During World War II, "As the champion of France rather than of any class or party, I incited hatred against no one and had no clientele who favored me in order to be favored in return."[5] The French President considers that he alone represents the community;

---

adroit to take the Minister of the Interior to task at a public meeting. They would have preferred to maintain the implicit 'nonaggression pact' which generally regulates official relations between communes and the state." Moreover, the conflict between the French government and the Association of Mayors has subsequently diminished. In December 1965 a delegation of the association was received by Prime Minister Pompidou and, in March and April 1966, by Minister of the Interior Frey. (See *Départements et communes* [December 1966], pp. 313–18; [April 1966], pp. 81–84.) On the fiftieth anniversary of the founding of the Association of Mayors, a delegation representing the association was received by President de Gaulle. (*Le Monde*, November 27–28, 1966.)

[3] Laurence Wylie, "Social Change at the Grass Roots," in Stanley Hoffmann, et al., *In Search of France* (Cambridge: Harvard University Press, 1963), p. 232. Wylie has noted the similar governing styles of Chanzeaux' traditional mayor and President de Gaulle in Wylie (ed.), *Chanzeaux: A Village in Anjou* (Cambridge: Harvard University Press, 1966), p. 229.

[4] See Chapter IX below, "The Rhetoric of *Apolitisme*," for a fuller discussion of the French mayor's conception.

[5] Charles de Gaulle, *The War Memoirs of Charles de Gaulle*, Vol. II: *Unity: 1942–44* (New York: Simon and Schuster, 1959), p. 271.

parliamentary institutions distort as much as they represent. In postwar France political parties at best commanded merely "an important fraction of citizens, not a single one was thought of as representing the public interest as a whole."[6] Consequently, de Gaulle relates, he had "to seek support from the French people rather than from the 'elite' groups which tended to come between us. . . ."[7] Like French mayors, General de Gaulle is disdainful of politics and of organized means of conducting political discussion. Parliamentary institutions may even be destructive: in discussing the Committee of National Liberation during the war, he concludes, "It must be added that without Parliament, elections, and parties, no politics were played among the members of the committee. My task of leadership was thereby facilitated."[8]

Although the regime and its mayors share a common approach to politics, they disagree on the constituency within which the apolitical style is to apply. Mayors see the commune as the natural unit. Local unanimity is required in order to resist encroachment from the outside world—and in this respect the state is the outsider *par excellence*. Gaullists see France, the French nation in its *grandeur*, as the proper object of devotion; loyalty to the commune is in that sense parochial and divisive. The French mayor's apolitical vision is thus transposed to the larger constituency.

The opposition of French mayors to the national government goes beyond particular questions of political parties or government policies. Its roots are to be found in the traditional

[6] *Ibid.*, Vol. III: *Salvation: 1944–46* (New York: Simon and Schuster, 1960), p. 272.

[7] *Ibid.*, III, 9.

[8] *Ibid.*, II, 136. The political style being elaborated resembles what Nicholas Wahl calls the administrative style; Wahl considers it a central feature of the French political character. (Wahl, "The French Political System," in Samuel H. Beer and Adam B. Ulam [eds.], *Patterns of Government*, 2nd ed. [New York: Random House, 1962], pp. 275–82; and *The Fifth Republic: France's New Political System* [New York: Random House, 1959], pp. 24–30.)

hostility of rural communities to strangers. Laurence Wylie has discussed Peyrane's generalized distrust of the outside world—the "they" which usually refers "to the French Government in all its manifestations. . . ."[9] For French farmers, "group cohesion appears to be essentially the awareness of forming a grouping opposed to the world of the city—an 'in group' opposed to an 'out group.' "[1] A similar description applies to the commune's stance toward the national government. The typical name of a slate in local elections is the List for the Defense of Local Interests.[2] Charles Brindillac asserts that the major task of the French mayor is to act as the commune's representative in dealing with the national government. "One doesn't ask a [French] mayor to know how to administer his commune. Rather, he is expected to be a skillful intermediary with the [government] authorities. . . ."[3] Brindillac's attack on French administration is entitled "Décoloniser la France." According to Brindillac, Frenchmen in the metropole were more tyrannized by their national administrative officials than were those people who lived under French colonial administration. He suggested, half seriously, that France study her system of colonial administration in Africa and Asia to learn how to improve her own administrative system.

A student of the Ecole Nationale d'Administration observes, "Basically, municipal authorities regard themselves less

[9] Laurence Wylie, *Village in the Vaucluse* (New York: Harper & Row, 1964), p. 205. Edward Banfield found villagers in southern Italy also to be distrustful of the outside world. (Banfield, *The Moral Basis of a Backward Society* [New York: The Free Press of Glencoe, 1958].)

[1] Jean Géraud and Gérard Spitzer, "Le Moral des agriculteurs," *Revue française de sociologie*, VI (1962), 5. See also Henri Mendras, *Sociologie de la campagne française* (Paris: Presses Universitaires de France, 1959), Chap. V.

[2] Charles d'Aragon, "Le Village et les pouvoirs," in Jacques Fauvet and Henri Mendras, *Les Paysans et la politique* (Paris: Armand Colin, 1958), p. 509. Also see Brian Chapman, *The Prefects and Provincial France* (London: George Allen & Unwin, 1955), pp. 192–93.

[3] Charles Brindillac, "Décoloniser la France," *Esprit*, XXV (December 1957), 802.

as the administrators of the commune than as its protectors, its intermediaries with the national administration."[4]

Local dependence on state financial support increases the difficulty of sponsoring municipal projects and intensifies the structural opposition between state and commune—although their opposition can also be traced to more general causes. The sponsorship of local projects demonstrates how mayoral actions are inextricably linked with the quest for communal harmony: a mayor weighs policies in the light of their possible effect on local unity. He carefully develops local support for his policies, partly by pointing to the need for communal solidarity against state interference. Mayors believe that their goals and interests conflict with those of the national government. Their suspicion toward the state stems from this belief yet, although justified, it appears to be exaggerated. The suspicion that mayors conspicuously display toward the state helps to maintain local unity, and it is this unity that is the overriding consideration. The manner in which local projects are sponsored in France becomes more explicable when viewed from the perspective of the attempt to maintain local consensus.

[4] Jacques Magnet, "Les Petites communes en Charente" (unpublished Mémoire, Ecole Nationale d'Administration, Paris, 1956), p. 10.

PART III

THE PLACE OF
POLITICS

Chapter VIII

How a Mayor Selects
His List

᙭ Free elections ordinarily represent an opportunity for opposition elements to organize and to challenge the incumbent
administration. One would therefore expect the appearance of
unity in most French communes to be threatened by municipal elections. Even if opposition lists are unsuccessful, one
might assume that their mere existence signifies a departure
from local unanimity.

However, a theory and practice of *apolitisme* help guarantee that even municipal elections will not significantly erode
local consensus. In most French communes local elections do
not constitute a meaningful challenge to local governmental
leadership. Prior to the local elections of 1959, one prefect
reported to the Minister of the Interior: "In 90 per cent of the
communes with a population of less than 1,000, citizens will
be faced with a single list."[1] In many cases, uncontested
local elections serve to symbolize the harmony that reigns in
the commune.

The pattern that one observer noted in French communes

[1] The Ministry of the Interior kindly made available reports written by
prefects to the ministry regarding the 1959 local elections. These will
hereafter be cited as "prefects' reports."

before World War II is still prevalent: "More often than not, local elections in tiny village communities are a mere formality. A slate is agreed upon in advance without opposition."[2]

Philip M. Williams summarizes the typical pattern of French local politics:

Most French towns have been ruled for years by a centre coalition, usually including and often led by the Socialists. Instead of a bitter conflict about the content of a joint programme—all the harder to agree on because it affirms principles which are unlikely to be realised—there is a common record of civic achievement to defend. Instead of a sordid squabble about the choice of candidates, there is a recognized leader, the existing mayor, often with a team [of incumbent municipal councilors] used to working together.[3]

In most communes the slate of candidates headed by the incumbent mayor is virtually unopposed. A study of mayors in a canton of the Sarthe found that, although in legislative elections there was a strong contest between left and right, with municipal councilors evenly divided between the two camps, "for local elections, only a single list runs in each commune; it is generally elected in its entirety."[4] When mayors face opposition, it is usually from a Communist list that stands little chance of victory and is regarded as illegitimate by most of the community. Julian Pitt-Rivers explains why only one list competed in local elections at Magnac:

No one else thinks it worthwhile to stand uninvited and in opposition. He would be certain to be outvoted and would be much

---

[2] Walter Rice Sharp, "Local Government in France," in William Anderson, *Local Government in Europe* (New York: Appleton-Century-Crofts, 1939), p. 129. Laurence Wylie discusses how the lack of overt opposition to Chanzeaux' local government was not equivalent to enthusiastic support. *Chanzeaux: A Village in Anjou* (Cambridge: Harvard University Press, 1966), Chaps. 10–12, and Conclusion.

[3] Philip M. Williams, "Party, Presidency and Parish Pump," *Parliamentary Affairs*, XVIII (Summer 1965), 261. See also Brian Chapman, *An Introduction to French Local Government* (London: George Allen & Unwin, 1953), p. 38.

[4] Jean de Nicolay, "Les Maires du canton de Montfort-le-Rotrou" (unpublished Mémoire, Institut d'Etudes Politiques de Paris, 1965), p. 31.

criticized by the majority as one who wished to sow discord in village affairs.[5]

For the 1959 local elections, *Le Monde* suggested that in many communes "the electorate can only choose between two lists, one Communist, with or without allies, the other a coalition [of all other political elements in the commune]."[6]

A mayor's list is likely to win in the forthcoming local election—and to win against little or no opposition. Consequently, being selected for the mayor's list is usually tantamount to being elected to the municipal council: a mayor virtually controls the composition of his commune's government. Since the composition of the slate plays a critical role in the preservation of local unity, the criteria that mayors use in selecting their list provide a key to understanding the bases of French local consensus.

A mayor chooses for his list those men (and occasionally women) who he believes will most effectively help to maintain communal unity. While few mayors run a serious risk of losing, no elected official is wholly immune to such fears. As *un tel maire* reflects to himself, "A vote, a simple majority vote can ruin my wildest dreams and take away or bestow the small kingdom I govern."[7] The mayor in the novel has little reason to fear defeat: after he has conducted a spirited election campaign and confessed great uncertainty about the outcome, his list still receives three-quarters of the popular vote. Yet, if for no other reason, the desire to secure re-election

[5] Julian Pitt-Rivers, "Social Class in a French Village," *Anthropological Quarterly*, XXXIII (January 1960), 8–9. For amusing incidents in the local elections of 1953, see Janet Flanner, *Paris Journal 1944–65* (New York: Atheneum, 1965), pp. 198–99.

[6] *Le Monde*, March 14, 1959.

[7] J.-L. Quereillahc, *Un tel . . . maire* (Paris: Editions France-Empire, 1962), p. 33. In the 1953 municipal elections, "the incumbent government in small and medium-size communes generally seems to have benefited from a sort of bonus given it by electors. This may be understandable in small communes where, even if the label changes, the municipal personnel is usually the same. But it is striking to note that even in the Paris industrial suburbs, the incumbent mayor, whether a Socialist or Communist, led his list to victory." (*Le Monde*, April 28, 1953.)

by an even higher margin than in the previous election will impel a mayor to select his running-mates with particular care.[8]

Mayors have a view of the commune and also a view of the municipal council's place in the commune. Their conception of the municipal council influences their selection of candidates for their list. What criteria guide a mayor in selecting candidates for his list? What are the characteristics of the men who are chosen for the mayor's list?

The most important force in the commune is the municipal council. A mayor is likely to begin the process of *dosage* (distribution of seats) by choosing candidates for his list who are already members of the municipal council: most men chosen for the mayor's list are likely to be incumbent councilors. Discussing the forthcoming 1959 local elections, a prefect observed, in reference to the communes in his department, "Often, about one-third of the time, a single list 'of local interests,' mostly composed of incumbent municipal councilors; in the other cases, two lists: one Communist, the second, a coalition list, based on the incumbent municipal council. . . ."[9]

Even when faced by an electoral challenge, incumbent councilors who seek re-election normally have excellent prospects for success. Laurence Wylie observes that for the 1953 municipal elections in Peyrane, two rival lists opposed each other, with the incumbent municipal councilors who were seeking re-election running together on one list. He examines which factors help explain the electoral result, but he does not stress the fact that five of the seven incumbents who were seeking re-election were successful.[1]

Wylie also describes a change in Chanzeaux' local political

---

[8] A Communist mayor spoke with pride of how he had increased his margin of victory between 1953 and 1959 by trying to please everyone, "opponents as well as friends."

[9] Prefects' reports.

[1] Laurence Wylie, *Village in the Vaucluse* (New York: Harper & Row, 1964), pp. 233–39. Peyrane's 1959 local election was more nearly typical

leadership resulting from the 1965 municipal election. Although the election produced an important change in the commune's leadership, the transition was facilitated in several ways: for example, the elderly mayor and six incumbent municipal councilors decided to retire rather than to seek re-election, the new councilors were in many respects (such as wealth) similar to the old, and the newcomers were among the more moderate of the challenging group. Moreover, while a majority of the newly elected thirteen-man municipal council had not served before, only one of the six incumbent municipal councilors who actually sought re-election was defeated.[2]

Although incumbent municipal councilors are *usually* re-elected, local electoral contests may occur and may result in the defeat of incumbents and a circulation of elites. In the example just cited, Chanzeaux' traditional political leaders were partially replaced by a younger and more dynamic group.[3] In most communes, however, the transition to new leadership is probably even more gradual and incomplete than at Chanzeaux, since the established coalition takes steps to prevent an open challenge to its dominance. Gordon Wright has pointed to a general transition toward younger rural leadership in France. He comments:

The full extent of this revolution in the 1959 municipal elections was concealed by the fact that a number of older politicians chose

---

of elections in most small communes than was the Peyrane local election of 1953. In 1959 the attempt was made to construct a slate acceptable to all political factions, headed by a candidate for mayor who was not associated with any one faction. The apolitical slate campaigned on the platform of being above politics. While the attempt to prevent competition failed and a rival slate was formed, nonetheless all candidates on the "apolitical" list were elected to the municipal council by large majorities. (*Ibid.*, pp. 353–63.)

[2] Wylie (ed.), *Chanzeaux, op. cit.*, p. 237.

[3] For a description of a power struggle in an unusual commune, see Henri Lefebvre, "Les Nouveaux ensembles urbains," *Revue française de sociologie*, I (April–June 1960), 186–201; and Lefebvre in Léo Hamon (ed.), *Les Nouveaux comportements politiques de la classe ouvrière* (Paris: Presses Universitaires de France, 1962), pp. 40–42.

*to co-opt young men for their own lists rather than face a rival
list of young activists.*[4]

When building a local coalition, it is not surprising for a
mayor to choose men for his list who were allies in former
local elections. However, he may also choose incumbent
councilors for his list who were elected from a rival list in
the previous election: several mayors said that they had
chosen former opponents for their lists. One mayor considered
it quite natural for all councilors to "fuse into a single group"
after the election, even if they had originally been elected from
different lists.

The informal process by which opposition elements on the
municipal council join forces and subsequently run together
for re-election is probably more common in small communes
than in large ones. Lists composed of former rivals in local
elections, however, are not unknown even in the very largest
French cities. Prior to the 1959 local election *Le Monde*
reported that the mayor of Bordeaux had persuaded incumbent
Radical, MRP, and Moderate councilors who had opposed
him in 1953 to join his list. Likewise, in preparation for the
1965 municipal election, the mayor of Bordeaux asked ten
opposition municipal councilors to join his list, of whom four
accepted.[5] In 1953 the mayor of Lille succeeded in forming a
list composed of the majority of incumbent municipal councilors—many of whom were his former opponents.[6] These
examples suggest the question of how, if former rivals in local
elections belong to different parties, they can subsequently
run together on the same list. The answer points to a significant and central feature of French local politics.

[4] Gordon Wright, *Rural Revolution in France* (Stanford, Calif.: Stanford
University Press, 1964), p. 159, note. Charles Roig also describes several
ways in which new leadership emerges at the local level, "L'Administration locale et les changements sociaux," in Institut d'Etudes Politiques
de Grenoble (ed.), *Administration traditionnelle et planification régionale*
(Paris: Armand Colin, 1964), pp. 67–68.
[5] *Le Monde*, March 4, 1959.
[6] *Le Monde*, March 4, 1965.

A typical mayor describes his list to the electorate as "composed of men devoted to the public good, who represent the political, economic, and social physiognomy of the community."[7] According to the mayor of France's sixth largest city, "My list . . . will unite men and women chosen because of their devotion and competence. It will assure the representation of all spiritual, political, and professional groups, as well as of our repatriated brothers [from Algeria]."[8] The mayor's most important criterion for choosing candidates for his list is to ensure that the municipal council will mirror the actual alignment of political forces in the commune as he interprets them. Since partisan affiliations are among the most significant divisions in a commune, balancing political party representation is a foremost aim. Mixed lists—composed of candidates from rival political parties—are a common characteristic of French municipal elections.

A mayor distributes seats on his list among political parties according to each party's importance in the commune. The proportion of seats on the coalition list allotted to representatives of a given political party is determined by the proportion of the commune's total vote cast for that party in the previous legislative elections. With an exception to be discussed below, the list that the mayor selects is thus intended to resemble in miniature the political complexion of the commune.

When explaining the principle that guided the selection of candidates for his list, one mayor stated the typical objective with particular clarity: "It's necessary for every ideology to be represented on the municipal council to ensure that unity will prevail." Mayors voluntarily grant representation on the municipal council precisely in order that independent opinions about communal affairs will not be expressed. While representation on the municipal council is used to reward groups, these groups, in return, are implicitly expected to renounce

---

[7] Quereillahc, op. cit., p. 44.
[8] Jacques Chaban-Delmas, quoted in Le Monde, March 4, 1959.

the use of representation for their own ends.[9] Once each political current in the commune is given the representation
commensurate with the proportion of its local vote in national
elections, there would no longer seem to be any function performed by the local election itself. Mayors take great care to
balance party representation on their list because, paradoxically, they believe joint lists to be the most effective way to
avoid political conflicts.

The major reason for balancing all political opinions on
the municipal council is thus to exclude political divisions
from the commune. It is hoped that differences about municipal affairs will not destroy the facade of local unity. Moreover,
while it is expected that national political conflicts may cause
divisions at the local level, the aim is to prevent local conflicts
over national issues from disrupting the commune.[1] Since the
municipal council stands for the commune, the harmony of
candidates from opposing political parties running on a single
list both facilitates and symbolizes communal harmony on
local affairs. Such reasoning explains the apparently paradoxi-
cal yet effective technique of nullifying political differences in

[9] Philip Selznick's distinction of formal and informal cooptation is relevant—*TVA and the Grass Roots* (Berkeley: University of California
Press, 1953), pp. 13-16, and 259-61. In a French commune new elements are absorbed into the leadership structure to maintain the stability
of the local government. Judging from the conservative orientation of
most local governments, in Selznick's terms the cooptation remains merely
formal.

[1] Occasionally, however, there is spillover between national and local
cleavages. In Quereillahc, *op. cit.*, p. 227, several municipal councilors
(who had run on the mayor's slate) turn their back on the mayor after
he publicly supports the incumbent deputy for re-election. In a local
election in another town, several municipal councilors form a list opposing
the mayor's after he is elected deputy on a partisan ticket. (Christian
Pineau, *Mon Cher député* [Paris: Julliard, 1959], pp. 90-99.)

The direction of spillover can also be in the opposite direction. Christian Prieur, "La Campagne électorale dans l'Aveyron," in Maurice
Duverger, François Goguel, and Jean Touchard (eds.), *Les Elections
du 2 janvier 1956* (Paris: Armand Colin, 1957), pp. 330-31, relates
how a conflict between hamlets in a commune has repercussions in that
commune's national voting behavior.

the commune by granting them their full weight on the municipal council.[2]

The Communists generally constitute an exception to the intricate balancing procedure described thus far. One mayor, while asserting that he considered competence more important than political opinion when he chose candidates for his list, added "although not a Communist, *bien sûr.*" The Communists are an isolated marginal group in the commune and are not considered worthy of being given their due place on the municipal council. Pierre Belleville comments, "Ten years of electoral campaigns and propaganda have made *apolitisme* in municipal elections synonymous with anticommunism."[3]

Consequently, when a list is formed in opposition to the mayor's list, it is likely to be predominantly Communist. However, even Communists may participate in mixed lists. In a report to the Ministry of the Interior before the 1959 municipal elections, a prefect stated that in "some small communes, where a single list solicits the vote of the electorate, one or two men from the extreme left [Communists] are traditionally included among the candidates." A conservative mayor (a member of the Moderate Party) told of having chosen Communists for his list. One municipal councilor described how a Communist in his commune was traditionally

[2] Similar reasoning might explain President de Gaulle's claim, prior to the 1962 legislative elections, that, when he was in power, he "took [his] ministers, suiting the occasion, from all the political groups, each in its turn and without exception . . . ." Address of November 7, 1962, reprinted in *Major Addresses, Statements and Press Conferences of General Charles de Gaulle: May 19, 1958–January 31, 1964* (New York: French Embassy, n.d.), p. 202.

[3] Pierre Belleville, "Dimension politique des élections municipales," *Perspectives socialistes* (January 1959), p. 2. Until recently, French voters perceived the Communist party to be extremely isolated. See Philip E. Converse, "The Problem of Party Distance in Models of Voting Change," in M. Kent Jennings and L. Harmon Ziegler (eds.), *The Electoral Process* (Englewood Cliffs, N.J.: Prentice-Hall, 1966), pp. 189–93 and Footnote 21. However, political changes and the findings of public opinion polls (reported in *Le Monde*, March 15, 1967), suggest that the French left is becoming less divided.

elected to the municipal council. Although he was offered a place on the mayor's list the Communist councilor refused to run with the other incumbent municipal councilors. Instead, he would announce his independent candidacy, form an incomplete list (consisting only of himself), and run against the rest of the incumbent government. The mayor, in turn, would print his list of candidates' names with one name blank on the ballot. It was informally understood by the commune's voters who their choice for the blank space should be. In this way, the Communist was regularly elected to the municipal council as a write-in candidate on the mayor's list!

A mayor of a small commune, in which local branches of national political parties do not exist, generally has greater control over the distribution of seats for his list than a mayor of a large commune has.[4] He approaches personally those individuals whose political affiliations will serve to balance his list. Mayors said they preferred to choose the men who will represent a political party rather than leave the choice to party officials. For example, a Moderate mayor told how he hoped to include Socialists on his list in the forthcoming election. In the previous local election he had considered the possibility of including a Socialist; however, when he discussed the matter with the local Socialist chairman, the latter insisted that *he* be the Socialist candidate on the mayor's list. Because of personal animosity between the two men, the mayor refused. As a result, the Socialists sponsored their own list. Although the mayor's list was elected in its entirety, the mayor considered the mere existence of a rival non-Communist slate to be a personal failure. He related that in the forthcoming election he hoped to persuade some Socialists to join his coali-

[4] More research is needed on local branches of French political parties. At Vienne, for example, a city of more than 21,000 (when it was studied in 1955), although the Socialist Party was extremely strong in the city, there was only one Socialist section for the whole commune. See Pierre Clément and Nelly Xydias, *Vienne sur le Rhône* (Paris: Armand Colin, 1955), pp. 117–18.

tion. "I've approached several Socialists individually and asked
them to be on my list," he said. "But I still won't work through
the Socialist Party."

A study of small communes in the Nord reports that in
local elections there, candidates from different parties often
run on the same list. The author speculates that these coalitions probably do not exist in large cities because the party
organizations would prevent their members from joining such
lists.[5] One mayor agreed. "I can keep Socialists on my list
because there isn't a Socialist section in a small village like
this, and therefore things are more fluid. A Socialist candidate
can run on my list without directly opposing his party."

Yet examination of the political composition of lists competing in local elections throughout France reveals that even
in large cities, mixed lists are not unusual.[6] While several lists
contest local elections in a large city, each list is frequently
a coalition of several political parties. Moreover, in a large
city's municipal election, a given political party is often represented on more than one list. Some mayors admitted that they
chose only "political friends" for their list. But more usual
was the 1959 municipal election in Poissy (near Paris), where
two Communist municipal councilors opposed a Communist
list and ran on a coalition list composed mainly of incumbent
councilors; and the 1959 municipal election in Dunkerque
(Nord), in which the incumbent Socialist mayor headed a
Radical-MRP-Moderate list—and won—against an all-Socialist
list.[7]

Municipal elections in large cities differ from municipal
elections in small towns; yet mixed lists are a common charac-

[5] René Rey, "Situation et avenir de la petite commune du Nord" (unpublished Mémoire, Ecole Nationale d'Administration, 1958), p. 6.
[6] The Bureau of Elections, Ministry of the Interior, kindly permitted me
to examine unpublished figures on municipal elections for all large cities
in France.
[7] Both examples taken from prefects' reports. The electoral law regulating
the 1965 municipal elections in cities over 30,000 also contributed to the
formation of urban political coalitions.

teristic of French municipal elections, whether in large cities or tiny communes. Local political coalitions play a critical role in shaping the character of French municipal politics.

In addition to political parties, other factors are also represented on the dominant list in small-town local elections. Mayors attempt to minimize geographic and class cleavages within the commune by coopting candidates from the commune's different geographic sections and occupational groups. At Vienne, "All parties seem to try, more or less successfully, to present lists which, if not balanced, at least include representatives from all socio-professional groups."[8] The mayor's list does not, however, reflect faithfully occupational distributions in the commune. A mayor believes that the wealthier elements in his commune should be given greater representation on the municipal council than their numbers alone would suggest. On the other hand, even if a mayor chooses only a few members of the working class for his list, he will probably feel that his actions demonstrate unusual sensitivity to the commune's political currents. One mayor proudly related that he had chosen two members of the working class for his list and that they had received as many votes as the other candidates he had chosen. Another mayor said that for the previous local election he had ignored workers who lived in the commune, and he now regarded this as an error. He was attempting to remedy an imbalance on the municipal council by inviting several workers to join the list he was preparing for the forthcoming local election.

More generally, the system of cooptation that is prevalent in most French communes consistently tends to underrepresent the lower class. Lucien Bernot and René Blancard compared the class composition of the Nouville municipal council

[8] Clément and Xydias, op. cit., p. 129. Parties in medium sized cities were encouraged to present separate lists at this time (1953 local elections) because of the system of proportional representation in cities over 9,000.

with the class composition of the commune and found that
farmers were represented on the municipal council far out of
proportion to their actual numbers, while workers were greatly
underrepresented.[9] In the rural canton studied by Marcel Jollivet, prosperous farmers and other wealthy citizens were generally overrepresented in elected positions, especially in local
offices. Of the 112 municipal councilors from the ten communes of the canton, 94 were farmers or farm workers.
Wealthy farmers were especially overrepresented: less than
2 per cent of the canton's farm workers were elected to the
municipal council, compared with more than 10 per cent of the
small farmers, one-half of the large farmers, and all five of
the very wealthy farmers. The author reports that an even
greater disproportion of mayors than municipal councilors are
wealthy.[1] "At Neuvic [Dordogne], a working-class city, there
are five farmers on the municipal council, compared to only
one foreman and one factory worker."[2] In the area studied by
Robert Arambourou, wealthy farmers monopolize the leading
positions in local government.[3] At Vienne, "the middle class
and lower middle class are overrepresented, compared to the
underrepresentation of the working class."[4] Although 38.5 per
cent of the total population of the city belonged to the working class, only 11.1 per cent of the municipal council were
workers. By contrast, the proportion of the salaried class on
the municipal council was nearly twice as high as in the gen-

[9] Lucien Bernot and René Blancard, Nouville, un village français (Travaux
et Mémoires de l'Institut d'Ethnologie, LVII; University of Paris, 1953),
p. 242.
[1] Marcel Jollivet, "Le Canton d'Orgères-en-Beauce," in Jacques Fauvet
and Henri Mendras, Les Paysans et la politique (Paris: Armand Colin,
1958), p. 458. See also Lucien Gachon, "L'Arrondissement d'Ambert,"
in ibid., p. 408.
[2] Thierry de Beaucé, "Opinions et attitudes des maires ruraux" (unpublished Mémoire, Institut d'Etudes Politiques de Paris, 1964), p. 24.
[3] Robert Arambourou, "La Gavacherie de Montségur," in François
Goguel (ed.), Nouvelles études de sociologie électorale (Paris: Armand
Colin, 1954), p. 113.
[4] Clément and Xydias, op. cit., p. 129.

eral population, and the proportion of professionals and industrialists on the municipal council was over five times higher
than in the general population.[5] Systematic underrepresentation of the lower class reinforces the conservative character
of French local politics.

Admittedly, in most political systems classes are not represented in strict proportion to their number. According to
Donald R. Matthews, "While the exact picture varies from
society to society and from time to time, we have found that
they [political leaders] tend to come from near the top of
society's system of social stratification."[6] However, in many
other cases—but rarely for French local politics—competition
between elites helps compensate for the lack of class balance
within the elite.

Aside from class cleavage, an important division in many
French communes is that between farmers and the inhabitants
of the commune's hamlets. Once again, however, the process
of cooptation helps to prevent conflict between the two forces.
When a mayor was asked, "Are there quarrels of hamlets
[against farmers] within the commune?" he replied, "No, one
tries to choose councilors from all over." Another mayor said,
"My assistant mayor is a farmer. That prevents a more open
struggle [between hamlet and rural area] and even possibly
a separate list."

In addition to trying to represent groups in their "proper"
proportion, a mayor chooses candidates who are assets to his
list because of their personal qualities and status in the community. One mayor said that he looked for "men of value,"
another for "qualified men." Laurence Wylie suggests that a
candidate's personality was the chief factor explaining success
or failure in the 1953 municipal elections at Peyrane. The
victors were *sérieux*, "the kind of men who are never accused

[5] *Ibid.*, p. 127.
[6] Donald R. Matthews, *The Social Background of Political Decision-
Makers* (New York: Random House, 1954), p. 56.

of prying into what does not concern them."[7] A mayor selects candidates with character and capacity, as well as those who represent political and social currents in the commune. In practice, however, emphasis on personal traits reinforces previous tendencies. At Chanzeaux, traditionally the chief qualifications for municipal councilors "were not their ideas, dynamism, or interest in the welfare of the commune; their seats on the council were the rewards for their economic success and social conformity."[8] As in most French communes, Chanzeaux' municipal councilors "were a choice group of the most conservative elements in the population."[9]

A mayor's attempt to build a joint list for local elections culminates in a coalition of political and social forces unknown in French national politics. The commune's unity is symbolized by a pre-election agreement on candidates for local office. The process that mayors follow to achieve electoral harmony resembles "ticket-balancing" in American politics. An important difference is that in most French communes voters are asked merely to ratify the result rather than to choose between two balanced tickets. Moreover, the strongly partisan nature of French national politics makes even more surprising the apolitical style that is characteristic of French local politics.

A mayor does not want different viewpoints or interests to be independently represented on the municipal council. Instead, by including candidates from among the commune's various elements a mayor seems to aim at blurring local political cleavages. The distinction may seem to be a fine one, but it is terribly real.

In order to preserve French local consensus, mayors try to prevent conflicts from occurring and differences from being expressed. Paradoxically, mayors feel that their ends can best

[7] Wylie, *Village in the Vaucluse, op. cit.*, p. 238. See also *Chanzeaux, op. cit.*, pp. 196, 207.
[8] *Ibid.*, p. 231.
[9] *Ibid.*, p. 229.

be served by accepting the legitimacy of each element's claim to representation. In return for this—so the implicit bargain seems to read—the various elements in the commune should agree to be satisfied with the recognition accorded them and should agree to suppress their particular claims.[1]

The extent to which the commune honors the bargain can be measured by the coalition lists in French local elections, the relatively slight competition in these elections, and the long tenure of French mayors. A high proportion of Frenchmen vote in local elections; yet the aim of most voters is to register satisfaction with the incumbent administration rather than to "throw the rascals out." As with municipal council unanimity, high turnout in local elections—especially when only one list stands a serious chance of winning—serves to symbolize the united commune. President de Gaulle expressed this attitude toward voting when, in discussing the impending referendum launching the Fifth Republic, he said, "The majority, or, as they say, the percentage of affirmative votes, will be of tremendous importance. Who then would want to abstain?"[2] Robert E. Lane suggests that citizens "who vote to show their solidarity with the dominant group can do so equally well [perhaps even better, one is tempted to add] in ritualistic elections. . . ."[3]

---

[1] See the excellent article by Belleville, op. cit., for a discussion of how the prevalence of apolitical lists in local elections minimizes local government activity. In "L'Eternal marais, essai sur le centrisme français," Revue française de science politique, XIV (February 1964), 33–51; and La Démocratie sans le peuple (Paris: Editions du Seuil, 1967); Maurice Duverger suggests that the characteristic centrisme of French national politics has permitted France to surmount otherwise irreconcilable extremes—but centrisme has also had the effect of preventing vigorous government activity. Cf. Swedish politics, as described by Dankwart A. Rustow, characterized by compromise, consensus—and conservatism (Rustow, The Politics of Compromise [Princeton, N.J.: Princeton University Press, 1955], Chap. VIII).

[2] Major Addresses, Statements and Press Conferences of General Charles de Gaulle: May 19, 1958–January 31, 1964, op. cit., p. 17.

[3] Robert E. Lane, Political Life: Why and How People Get Involved in Politics (New York: The Free Press of Glencoe, 1959), p. 309.

The method that mayors use to select candidates for their list underlies local consensus. Moreover, the apolitical method is accompanied by a rhetoric characteristic of French local government: the rhetoric of *apolitisme* legitimizes a practice that might otherwise be regarded as undemocratic.

Chapter IX

The Rhetoric of *Apolitisme*

Mayors insist that they do not make choices—and certainly not political choices—during the performance of their official duties. One said:

The area needs projects, achievements. That's not politics. Where projects are concerned, there's unanimity in the commune. We have different political opinions, but in the commune there's always unanimity. And that's also true for the municipal council.

A Socialist deputy mayor unknowingly repeated the classic argument used by the American municipal reform movement to oppose politics when he said, "For the problem of water, schools and roads, there's no Gaullist view and no Communist view. I don't see any reason for the injection of politics. Everyone should agree."

A Radical mayor who was president of his department's Radical federation concurred: "There aren't fifty ways to administer a commune. When responsible men study the needs of the commune, they agree on what should be done. It's not a party matter."

The most frequently heard claim a mayor makes is, "*Je ne fais pas de politique* [I don't engage in politics]." According to one mayor, "The commune's interest is so vast that it surpasses our political differences."[1] A municipal councilor replied, when asked if political considerations were important at municipal council meetings:

There are no political differences within the municipal council. It's just that differences spring from different opinions about administration. Someone may want a Salle des Fêtes, while others may prefer to save the money.

A former mayor reviewed his difficulties in administering Issy-les-Moulineaux, an industrial suburb near Paris. He discussed several projects which had created great local controversy, such as sponsoring municipal housing construction and expanding the municipal library. Yet after summarizing his constituents' extremely divergent opinions about how the commune should be administered, he concluded, "There are not several ways to administer a commune correctly."[2]

When mayors deny that their role is political, they do not mean that political considerations are irrelevant to the conduct of local office. For example, summarizing the manner in which he chose his running mates in local elections, one mayor said that he was careful "to represent the political composition of the commune—from left to right." When a mayor says that political considerations do not influence his behavior in local politics, he means that he is impartial—that he does not favor a given interest, opinion, or political party—including his own. One mayor explained, "A mayor's job isn't political. He treats everyone in the same way."

One mayor general councilor said that his commune had no difficulty obtaining grants from the department for local roads because the general councilor of the neighboring canton was president of the general council's road commission. When

---

[1] Quoted in Thierry de Beaucé, "Opinions et attitudes des maires ruraux: (unpublished Mémoire, Institut d'Etudes Politiques de Paris, 1964), p. 89.

[2] Jacques Madaule, "Quatre ans de mairie," *Esprit*, XXI (May 1953), 780.

asked if there was much political bargaining in the general council, he replied, "That's not politics. It's a question of who holds powerful positions and who one's friends are."

To a French mayor, "politics" means, in part, giving weight to partisan considerations. Yet engaging in politics may not be considered illegitimate so long as it does not affect one's performance in local office. The last mayor cited seemed piqued when he was asked subsequently if he engaged in national politics. "Why yes," he replied, "that's natural, isn't it?"[3]

A mayor may be involved in politics and feel that his involvement is entirely acceptable. Yet, as mayor, he believes himself obligated to prevent political considerations from intruding into communal affairs. A Socialist mayor, who was also a deputy and vice-chairman of the Socialist parliamentary party, asserted, in quite un-Marxian fashion, "A mayor should strive for unity in his commune. It isn't good to have divisions. He should represent everyone and avoid cutting the commune into two or three parts."

A deputy mayor suggested that his occupying a prominent position enabled him to help his commune. However, he denied that politics played a part: "It's just that whoever has more power gets more done."

Mayors might be accused of resorting to what Marcel Merle has called "tactical *apolitisme*," whose slogan is:

"Vote for me because I don't engage in politics." The party or candidate that uses this argument isn't really trying to destroy political activity: in fact, the argument is used to solicit votes according to the classic rules of the political game. The aim is to obtain or keep an elected position.[4]

The complexity of the concept *apolitisme* is noted by another scholar:

[3] In a public opinion poll, one-fourth of the French considered politics to be inherently dishonorable. *Sondages*, XXV (1963), 108.
[4] Marcel Merle, "Inventaire des apolitismes en France," in Georges Vedel (ed.), *La Dépolitisation: mythe ou réalité?* (Paris: Armand Colin, 1962), p. 43.

The term apolitisme *is ambiguous and obscure. It is ambiguous when it is used by politicians.* When *politicians claim that they are pursuing apolitical ends, they mean that these ends are in the public interest and are not partisan. One may, nevertheless, wonder if by proclaiming their* apolitisme *they are not consciously or unconsciously seeking to hide the partisan character of their efforts.*[5]

The apolitical claim has been made often in the national political arena. In discussing the November 1962 legislative elections, one observer noted ironically, "The Gaullist triumph is that of men who *ne font pas de politique* [do not engage in politics]...."[6]

Part of the difficulty may arise from the French language itself. According to Léo Hamon, *la politique* can mean:

1. The management of public affairs. (The English equivalent would be "policy.")
2. More narrowly, competition between factions, each offering solutions to various questions. (Hamon suggests that this corresponds to the English "politics.")
3. More narrow still, the concrete competition between existing groups at a given moment.[7]

Yet adopting a position of linguistic determinism does not appear to resolve the problem. In English, too, there is an ambiguity in the word "politics," which has both a value-neutral and a pejorative connotation. French mayors do not

[5] Pierre Fougeyrollas, *La Conscience politique dans la France contemporaine* (Paris: Editions Denoël, 1963), p. 236, in the section entitled "La Question de l'apolitisme et de la dépolitisation," pp. 235–52. See also Francis Houdet, "Vie locale et vie politique," *Citoyens* "60," no. 7 (Oct.–Nov. 1961), p. 13; and *Esprit*, XXVII (January 1959), 129–32.
[6] Roger Ikor, "Au temps de marécage," *Démocratie 62*, no. 162 (November 29, 1962); quoted by Fougeyrollas, *op. cit.*, p. 250. Also see the remark by Pierre-Henri Teitgen, in Colloque 'France-Forum' (ed.), *La Démocratie à refaire* (Paris: Les Editions Ouvrières, 1963), p. 48.
[7] Léo Hamon, "Partis politiques et dépolitisation," in Vedel (ed.), *op. cit.*, p. 145. Jean Rivero also discusses the semantic difficulty, *ibid.*, p. 162. The ambiguity of the term was used to defend General Zeller's participation in the "revolt of the generals" in April 1961. (Edgar Furniss, Jr., *De Gaulle and the French Army* [New York: The Twentieth Century Fund, 1964], p. 65.)

merely assert that partisan affiliations should not affect the resolution of local issues; they also believe that the commune should not be divided by differences over *policies*.

The rhetoric of *apolitisme* underlies French local government. Mayors assert that their commune should not be divided because its natural condition is one of unity. But an important reason for the absence of municipal conflicts is that mayors exert careful effort to prevent divisions from arising. Once they are successful in convincing others, mayors can attribute the lack of conflict in their communes to the validity of the rhetoric.

Does the lack of competition characteristic of French local government represent a genuine harmony of communal interests? Is the absence of organized opposition to local governments due to the absence of political cleavages and conflicts of interest within the commune? Are mayors correct in asserting that their tasks are nonpolitical and that political judgments do not play a part in their decisions?

If there were no important conflicts of interest on local issues within a commune, the commune might belong to the realm of the subpolitical. One might assert that a local government hardly has the financial, legal, or political power to affect the destinies of the commune's inhabitants. Local governments can do relatively little and what they do is largely routine. Consequently, mayors would be correct in asserting that political divisions are not appropriate to local government. Especially if one believed the rhetoric of *apolitisme*, one might agree that the commune is more like a family than a state. As Aristotle noted:

Is it not obvious that a state may at length attain such a degree of unity as to be no longer a state?—since the nature of a state is to be a plurality, and in tending to great unity, from being a state, it becomes a family. . . .[8]

[8] Aristotle, *Politics*, ii. 2, trans. by Benjamin Jowett (New York: The Modern Library, 1943), p. 81.

And yet the lack of organized opposition to the local government does not prove that conflicts of interest do not exist within the commune.[9] To paraphrase Marx, in *The Eighteenth Brumaire*, men may choose but they do not choose under completely free circumstances. A situation is shaped by its existing possibilities. If citizens are offered only one meaningful possibility, it is doubtful whether they will perceive the absence of other alternatives.

Two mayors in adjoining communes near Bordeaux told how each had sponsored the construction of an elementary school in his commune. Brinsac's new school was built in stages.[1] Every several years another addition was added to the developing school; the whole school took ten years to complete. When asked why the school had been built in this manner, Brinsac's mayor explained that the procedure permitted Brinsac to benefit from its school soon after construction began. Although the local government did not have sufficient funds to build the whole school at once, Brinsac was able to use the portion of the school that had already been completed.

Moreover, the commune was able to receive public support sooner by this method. The general council subsidized school construction provided its cost was below a specified limit; if the cost of a proposed school exceeded that limit, a commune had to apply to the national government for a grant.[2] Each stage of construction of Brinsac's school cost less than the limit established by the general council. As a result, the commune received a grant from the general council every few

[9] At Chanzeaux, Laurence Wylie suggests that, despite the surface impression, the commune has been characterized by diversity and disunity rather than by homogeneity and harmony. (Wylie [ed.], *Chanzeaux: A Village in Anjou* [Cambridge: Harvard University Press, 1966], pp. 334 ff.)

[1] The names of the communes are fictitious.

[2] There are three categories of educational construction projects: repairs and small construction projects, both of which are subsidized by departmental grants, and major projects, financed in part by grants from the national government.

years to help finance construction of the next stage. "And just look at Le Targon [the neighboring commune]," triumphantly concluded the mayor. "They only got their school last year."

The mayor of Le Targon felt very differently about the outcome. "You see this school?" he said proudly. "It's bigger and much more beautiful than Brinsac's school. I waited until we could get a grant from the national government in Paris before building my school, not like Brinsac."

Le Targon did indeed appear to have a better school. It had applied to the national government for a school-construction grant, because the total cost of its school exceeded projects that the general council subsidized. Le Targon had to manage with its old school for several additional years but, when it finally received the state grant, the amount was sufficient to permit Le Targon to undertake a major project of school construction. The dilemma thus was that, while the general council would provide small grants in a relatively short time, if one wanted to obtain a larger state grant, one would have to be prepared to wait.

Which commune had made the wiser choice? The answer, of course, depends on many factors—how urgently a school was needed, the financial resources of the communes, the difference in the grants accorded by the department and the state, and the quality of the two types of construction. But in addition to these apparently technical questions, a final decision is influenced by political values. Is a bird in the hand at Brinsac worth two in the bush at Le Targon?

In neither commune were the citizens given the opportunity to decide. In each commune, the decision was made by the mayor, without any public discussion of the alternatives that faced the commune.

One need not share the political views of one Communist mayor to agree that possibilities for choice exist at different political levels:

The bourgeois cast politics in a bad light so workers won't engage in politics. But politics is the art of organizing the economy of a unit. At each political level one organizes the economy according to one's principles. As a Communist, I do things differently from other mayors.

The local government presided over by the Communist mayor operated its own municipal services for many functions —for example, garbage collection and road maintenance. Local governments in other communes contracted with private companies for these services to be operated as concessions. The Communist mayor's local government also sponsored public services that were rarely found in comparable communes: a recreation center for elderly residents and one for young people, low-cost public housing, and a municipal library. The Communist mayor did not levy several local taxes that are apportioned without regard to income—for example, taxes on drainage and garbage collection. Instead, he levied to the maximum permissible limit a progressive tax on real estate and industry, which therefore fell more heavily on large landowners and manufacturers in the commune.

Likewise at Aubervilliers, a Communist suburb of Paris, when local taxes are raised it is "on the basis of the class principle of our [Communist] party—*make the rich pay*. In practice this means an increase affecting industrialists proportionately more than workers."[3] An article about the Paris "red belt" finds that Communist mayors have a unique governing style; for example, they are especially apt to sponsor cultural and welfare facilities.[4]

Yet not even all Communist mayors are as quick to stress the political character of their position. In one canton, all

[3] Henri Chauveau, "Le Rôle de plus en plus important des municipalités," *Cahiers du communisme*, XLI (February 1965), 12. (Italics in original.)
[4] Paul Thibaud, "Le Communisme municipal," *Esprit*, XXXIV (October 1966), 413–22. See also Jacques Duclos, "Les Municipalités Communistes au service des populations," *Nouvelle revue internationale*, IX (May 1966), 89–99.

mayors agreed their position was apolitical. "The single Communist mayor, although admitting his position involved a political aspect, asserted 'that it is only political far after everything else.' "[5] A Communist mayor in another region said, "We are administrators who become politicians only during election campaigns. Afterwards, we again become administrators for everyone."[6]

An article discussing how Socialists can influence municipal policy suggests the range of possibilities open to French local governments: when Socialists are in the minority on the municipal council, they can try to block unfavorable measures; when they control the local government, the commune can sponsor public housing, health clinics, and other municipal facilities.[7] Another study of French communes suggests that local governments can be either *conservatrice, sociale,* or *dynamique.*[8] A prefect's chief aide observed, "Several communes have been rejuvenated with a new mayor. Others strangle, despite their resources, because their mayor is too old."[9] One mayor stated wryly, "You can't be blamed if you only do what you have to do."[1]

Local governments use their powers in widely differing ways. There are manifold possibilities for action. Some communes have a high local tax rate and a variety of public services; in other communes the tax rate is lower, and there

[5] Hélie de Noailles, "Le Maire face aux problèmes communaux dans la région parisienne" (unpublished Mémoire, Institut d'Etudes Politiques de Paris, 1964), p. 22.
[6] Thierry de Beaucé, "Opinions et attitudes des maires ruraux" (unpublished Mémoire, Institut d'Etudes Politiques de Paris, 1964), p. 41.
[7] J. Ries, "Socialisme et vie municipale," *La Revue socialiste,* no. 66 (April 1953), pp. 352–72. See also *Municipalités et politique,* a series of articles in *Perspectives socialistes* (January 1959).
[8] Roger Aubin, *Communes et démocratie, I: taches et moyens de la commune* (Paris: Les Editions Ouvrières, 1965), pp. 218–20. See also L. Stehelin, *Essais de socialisme municipal* (Paris: Librarie de la Société du Recueil Général des Lois . . ., 1901).
[9] De Beaucé, *op. cit.,* p. 60.
[1] *Ibid.,* p. 37.

are fewer public facilities. Some communes provide school children with free textbooks, subsidized noonday meals, and bus transportation. In other communes either these services are not provided at all or else their cost is borne directly by the families of the school children.[2]

According to Jean Hourticq, post-war administrative decrees "permitted communes to do practically anything they want, provided they have the financial means, the political authority, and the necessary personnel."[3] Local governments

[2] See the article by Henri Fréville, deputy and mayor of Rennes, in which the vast possibilities for municipal action are discussed. Fréville, "Un maire, responsable de la cité," in Hervé Carrier and Philippe Laurent (eds.), Le Phénomène urbain (Paris: Aubier-Montaigne, 1965), pp. 181–95. For a description of Fréville's achievements as mayor, see Claude Cattaert, "Un Apôtre de l'action," Réalités, no. 194 (March 1962), 62–67. M. Tézier, another French mayor discusses how he fostered local development in, "L'Expansion par industrialisation, l'exemple de Voiron," Etude des problèmes municipaux, no. 7 (September 1965), pp. 24–26. Christian Rudel reviews how local action can be fostered in Mon Village à l'heure de l'expansion (Paris: Les Editions Ouvrières, 1965). Balzac's novel, Le Médicin de campagne, describes a mayor who transformed his commune: as the result of sponsoring road and housing construction, attracting commerce and industry, and introducing new agricultural techniques, the population of the commune rose from 700 to 2,000 in a decade.

[3] Jean Hourticq, "L'Administration et la vie locale" (Mimeographed course notes, Institut d'Etudes Politiques de Paris, 1963–64), p. 393; and see also G. Maleville, "Le Décret no. 55–579 du 20 mai 1955," Départements et communes (July–August 1955), p. 223. In discussing "The Areal Division of Powers in the Writings of French Political Thinkers" (in Arthur Maass [ed.], Area and Power: A Theory of Local Government [Glencoe, Ill.: The Free Press, 1959], p. 139), Stanley Hoffmann minimizes the independence of French local government: "The powers of the territorial units are purely administrative, limited to the implementation of the laws voted at the center, which express and monopolize the general will." (See also, ibid., p. 148, Footnote 65.) However, according to Charles Roig, "Théorie et réalité de la décentralisation," Revue française de science politique, XVI (June 1966), 464, "One must beware of an overly normative interpretation of administrative regulations, for they portray a false conception of French local government. 'Decentralization' is not merely the margin of formal liberty left to local officials; it includes also the liberty of action local officials achieve by interpreting, evading, or ignoring the texts. French local government is characterized less by centralization than by the maintenance of the status quo due to regional neutrality or tacit complicity between central and local authorities."

may choose to exercise their powers in ways that will either sustain or change established communal social patterns. Some communes, for example, have sponsored low-cost day nurseries for preschool age children. One mayor opposed these nurseries because he believed that they produced what he considered harmful social effects: a mother sends her children to the nursery so that she can be free during the day to take a job. The mayor did not want the local government to make it easier for traditional family habits to be changed.[4] Another mayor believed that the real difficulty was low family incomes. He felt that a municipally operated day nursery was beneficial because it freed mothers to work, thus providing an opportunity for families to supplement their incomes, while ensuring that children received proper care.

By their actions, if not by their words, mayors demonstrate that politics is relevant to the commune. A local government makes choices, and these choices have consequences for residents of the commune. Communal resources can be distributed in various ways, in accordance with the political values of those who decide local governmental policy. The choice of projects, their priorities, and how they will be undertaken might all lend themselves to political discussion. Joseph Barthélemy has observed:

The mayor is sometimes described as an arbiter, a paternal authority above political parties. . . . This is pure fiction: municipal elections are a political struggle; the mayor is the leader of the winning party. He is therefore committed to his party and cannot be expected to be impartial.[5]

Political differences and conflicts of interest exist within French communes as they do within any public group. The major difference between French communes and other demo-

---

[4] Laurence Wylie points out that one of the traditional aims of local government was to protect the family unit. (*Chanzeaux, op. cit.*, p. 239.)
[5] Joseph Barthélemy, *Le Gouvernement de la France*, 2nd ed. (Paris: Payot, 1939), p. 171.

cratic constituencies is that there is little opportunity in the commune for these differences and conflicts to become manifest.

The rhetoric of *apolitisme* has had a conservative influence on French local government: it discourages the articulation of grievances against those in power, and permits the locally powerful to coopt those who might otherwise form an organized opposition to incumbent leaders.

Occasionally, the established doctrine is questioned. Before the 1959 local elections a worker in Le Havre explained why he would not vote for the incumbent mayor for re-election: "When he put in street lighting, he forgot about the working-class neighborhoods."[6] One mayor interviewed said that his predecessor had been defeated for re-election because he was regarded as selfish. Since he himself already had a private well sufficient for his own family's needs, he refused to permit the commune's participation in an intercommunal association which would provide running water for homes in the area. Despite the fact that many of his neighbors did not have running water, he did not want to pay the additional taxes that membership in the association would entail. The intercommunal association would be able to provide an adequate water supply for the member communes. It would pool the tax resources of several communes along with loans and grants from the state. A large well would be built to feed water into a storage tank; the water stored in the tank would then be piped to all homes in the region, thus permitting many homes to have indoor running water for the first time.

The former mayor did not join the association because, if he did so, the town's taxes would have to be raised. Most residents of the commune resented the fact that their mayor put low taxes ahead of the commune's welfare. They rebelled against his leadership and defeated him for re-election to the

[6] Claude Estier, "La Teste électorale du Havre," *France Observateur* (March 5, 1959), p. 4.

municipal council.[7] However, this case is unusual: most mayors would have been aware of their neighbors' resentment and would not have so blatantly placed their own personal interest ahead of the community interest. Moreover, even if a mayor were to act selfishly, a community-wide revolt would be unlikely.

One might argue, as do many mayors, that conflicts over local issues disrupt the commune, and that it is wrong for neighbors to disagree about local matters. If communal harmony requires the absence of some democratic trappings, nonetheless, the implicit argument goes, this is a price well worth paying.

Perhaps the doctrine should not be rejected simply because of its obviously self-serving character. It *is* possible that French communes might be deeply split if cleavages over local matters were to reinforce already existing cleavages over national political issues. Yet the argument assumes that French communes are in a relatively satisfactory position; the case is not proved, however, by pointing to the absence of overt opposition to most local governments. The widespread emigration from many French communes suggests that young Frenchmen are voting with their feet.[8] More active French local governments in small communes might offer their citizens a measure of urban amenities, without giving up the advantages of rural life.[9] A more vigorously functioning local democratic system might mobilize citizens to improve local conditions rather than

[7] For other examples of revolts against local leadership, see pp. 123–24 and the references cited there.

[8] At Chanzeaux and Peyrane, asserts Laurence Wylie, dissatisfaction with possibilities locally is responsible for the exodus of the most talented young people in the community. (*Village in the Vaucluse* [New York: Harper & Row, 1964], pp. 336–37; and *Chanzeaux* [*op. cit.*], p. 336.)

[9] In a public opinion poll French citizens registered their belief that, as compared with their general councilor, deputy, professional organization, and others, the local government defended regional interests best. However, when they were asked where the best hope for regional improvement lay, local government fell to fourth in popular opinion. "Les Agents de l'action régionale," *Sondages*, XXVII (1965), 69–71.

to seek improvements elsewhere. Dissident and discontented elements might channel their energies toward gaining control of local governments in order to use the government to achieve their goals.[1]

Instead, the ideology of *apolitisme* discourages the articulation of local differences. Harmony is preserved by adhering to a fictional view of the commune. Would local party competition be worth the risk of fragmenting the commune? The answer depends in part on one's own political convictions. Yet, perhaps more important, the question is rarely asked by French citizens or governors. In the French commune "politics as usual" means that political dialogue does not exist.

[1] In *Chanzeaux, op. cit.,* Chap. 12, Wylie describes how the youth of Chanzeaux' new municipal leadership will predispose them toward a more dynamic approach to local government. See also Gordon Wright, *Rural Revolution in France* (Stanford, Calif.: Stanford University Press, 1964), pp. 324–30, on the relationship between age and activism at the local level in France.

Chapter X

The Ambiguous Consensus

The greatest talent a ruler can possess is to disguise his power, in order to render it less odious, and to conduct the state so peaceably as to make it seem to have no need of conductors.[1]

What is the character of the consensus that prevails in French local politics? The mayor of a small French town can be compared to a *chef d'orchestre*. Each feels out all the possibilities in his ensemble; each is intimately familiar with the temperaments and the particular needs of all members. Walter Lippmann has also compared the body politic to an orchestra, in which a conductor is needed "to see to it that each man plays his part."[2]

In the commune the mayor moves within a context that is remarkably free of institutional restraints. While a mayor cannot completely ignore the interests and desires of his constituents, save for the relatively slight possibility of not being re-elected he has great latitude in interpreting citizen interests and allocating the resources of the local government.[3]

---

[1] Jean-Jacques Rousseau, "A Discourse on Political Economy," in *The Social Contract and Discourses*, trans. by G. D. H. Cole (New York: E. P. Dutton & Co., 1941), p. 258.
[2] Walter Lippmann, *Public Opinion* (New York: Macmillan, 1922), p. 264.
[3] There are restraints imposed on the mayor from outside the commune, but what is referred to here are the lack of restraints within the commune. Similarly, although the *chef d'orchestre* is all-powerful within the orchestra, he must deal with labor unions, the government, and others who limit his freedom.

One important reason for his freedom is the lack of an organized opposition. Local apathy is epitomized by the absence of competitive political parties on the municipal level. While some of the purposes that political parties traditionally serve are met in French local government, others are not. A party traditionally recruits leaders by nominating candidates for public office; it is the mayor who recruits local leaders in France. He selects candidates in an informal but carefully prescribed manner, welds the commune's leaders into one list and, on election day, presents it to the commune for its approval.

Another function that political parties traditionally perform is to present a program which the party pledges to implement if it is elected. In French communes the mayor and his candidates for the municipal council write a *profession de foi* (electoral program), which is distributed to the commune's voters.[4] The program indicates what the slate will accomplish if it is elected. The program deals with concrete projects in the community, such as building a sports field, paving certain roads, refurbishing the town hall. In its electoral program the incumbent administration enumerates its achievements since the previous election and specifies the amount in state grants that have been obtained for its projects.

However a party's program is meaningful only if voters can compare it with other programs. Unless there is more than one party, voters do not have a chance to choose among alternatives. Opposition parties are important because they mobilize dissatisfied elements in the community, articulate their grievances, and transform the discontent of individuals or groups into an alternative to the government's program. In response to the opposition, the majority party is induced to remain vigorous and alert. In short, opposition parties are essential to a democratic community. According to Ernest Barker:

[4] Two typical *professions de foi* are reproduced in Appendix C.

There must necessarily be a plurality of parties. A single party cannot provide the basis of a system of government by discussion. Discussion is ended at once if only a single issue is formulated and a single programme is enunciated.[5]

For Leslie Lipson:

The parties in a democratic regime survive or fall under the conditions of competition, and their political being is fundamentally altered when they live by challenging others and being challenged in turn.[6]

And V. O. Key observes:

If support for the minority rested solely on opinions grounded in particular issues, the life of the opposition would be precarious. Given the nature of governments, an opposition with stable popular foundations is a useful piece of equipment to have around.[7]

Yet an organized legitimate opposition is conspicuously lacking in most French communes. When there is a second list in local elections, it is usually Communist. But the Communist Party is not an effective agent for mobilizing discontent: the Communists are separate and isolated; their criticisms of the local government, however valid, are dismissed by most voters. The electoral system makes it difficult for a single group like the Communists to gain representation on the municipal council, even if the Communist list receives a significant proportion of the total vote. Communist criticism does not educate the commune or make the government more responsive.

Furthermore, in most small communes there is no other source from which informed criticism might come. For example, regional newspapers devote only brief space to each commune in the area. Most news in these local pages is about

[5] Ernest Barker, *Reflections on Government* (London: Oxford University Press, 1944), p. 39.
[6] Leslie Lipson, *The Democratic Civilization* (Princeton, N.J.: Princeton University Press, 1965), p. 311.
[7] V. O. Key, *Public Opinion and American Democracy* (New York: Alfred A. Knopf, 1964), p. 68.

social or sports events. When news is reported of local political issues, no editorial position is taken. Few organized groups in the commune direct pressure at the government. Consequently, only the mayor and his political machine are responsible for searching out discontent in the community and remedying it through political action. To the classic question—"who will watch the watchmen?"—the prevailing answer in French local government is that they will watch themselves.[8]

Yet it appears that most Frenchmen do find their local government satisfactory. Discussing the 1965 municipal election results, François Goguel observed, "The municipal elections demonstrated that in most cases French voters are satisfied with the way in which municipal affairs are administered in their commune."[9] With reference to the Fourth Republic Philip M. Williams notes, "In local government, for all its limited powers, there was a circuit of confidence between rulers and people. In the National Assembly, for all its omnipotence, there was none."[1] In Nouville, "even the greatest critics of the incumbent mayor realize he is indispensable."[2] Most Frenchmen treat their mayor with great respect. They regard him as an important figure, and feel honored when he chats with them. Citizens generally describe their mayor as a person of integrity and worth.

[8] Grant McConnell's criticism of private associations in the United States applies also to French local governments: "The institutions of their political systems provide few checks or limitations upon the power of leaders. Nor do they provide any but the most rudimentary means for taking account of the differences among members. On these scores, the principal restraint seems to lie in the leaders' intuitive capacity to perceive potential hostility that might result in rebellion." (*Private Power and American Democracy* [New York: Alfred A. Knopf, 1966], p. 342.) McConnell suggests that "the myth of unity" helps maintain the leadership in power. (*Ibid.*)

[9] François Goguel, "Les Elections municipales des 14 et 21 mars 1965: la signification de la consultation," *Revue française de science politique,* XV (October 1965), 916.

[1] Philip M. Williams, *Crisis and Compromise,* 3rd ed. (Hamden, Conn.: Shoe String Press, 1964), p. 332.

[2] Lucien Bernot and René Blancard, *Nouville, un village français* (Travaux et Mémoires de l'Institut d'Ethnologie, LVII; University of Paris, 1953), p. 25.

A major reason mayors retain local control is their commitment to their position. All mayors with whom interviews were conducted devote at least several hours each week to communal affairs. Only the town clerk spends as much time on matters relating to local government. While town clerks have been described as the dominant figures in local government, this evaluation appears to overestimate their actual power: the town clerk's expertise is less important than the mayor's personal authority.[3]

It is highly instructive to accompany a mayor when he tours his commune. A feeling of warmth, intimacy, and dignity strikes the outside observer. A mayor's visits to friends and neighbors appear purely social, for most of the conversation concerns personal news in the commune. However, these visits also serve the crucial political function of telling the mayor who in the commune wants what, when, and how much. No mayor is ever without his notebook; after visiting a constituent, he notes the items requiring his attention. When possible, mayors are prompt to satisfy constituents' requests.

A mayor's visits are an informal but highly effective way of discerning grievances and their remedies. With the information he has gained, the mayor is uniquely qualified to perform his job, for all else in the commune revolves around him. In the course of his visits, the mayor not only ascertains public opinion, he also molds it.

Morris Janowitz has questioned:

What would be the consequences if the major actors had a clearer understanding of the structures of community power in

[3] For the argument that the town clerk "is frequently the real manager of the community, even though the mayor remains the titular authority," see Laurence Wylie, *Village in the Vaucluse* (New York: Harper & Row, 1964), pp. 61–62; and Wylie in Stanley Hoffmann, *et al.*, *In Search of France* (Cambridge: Harvard University Press, 1963), pp. 219–21. For the contrary case, see Eric Degremont, *Les Maires ruraux, leur autorité* (unpublished Mémoire, Institut d'Etudes Politiques de Paris, 1964), p. 60.

*which they are involved? The prediction is that such knowledge
would enhance the processes of group representation and the
formulation of community consensus.*[4]

The French mayor has a certain understanding, one might
even say a certain vision, of his commune. In his view, the
commune is united in its interests: no difference exists that
cannot be resolved by patience and dedication to the communal good. There is no necessary conflict of interest within
the commune, whether of hamlet against rural area, of lower
class against middle class, or of Socialist against UNR.[5] Yet
the consensus that emerges from this vision is ambiguous.

Most political thinkers, such as Bentham, Madison, and
Bentley, have viewed representation as permitting groups to
compete with each other for their share of the political spoils.
Consensus is minimal and centers around the "rules of the
game" that govern conflict among groups. In French local government it is implicitly assumed that each group in the commune should be represented equitably by being given its due
weight on the municipal council. The purpose of this representation, however, is not to enable groups to compete with
each other for their share of the communal spoils; rather, each
group is given fair representation so that differences will not
be emphasized but nullified. In other words, the result of
representation should not be the competition of each against
each, but rather communal harmony, where there will be no
strife whatsoever. Harmony does not result from groups competing with each other according to specified rules but from a
tacit understanding that competition will not occur. Representation on the municipal council is thus intended to obviate
the need for struggle. A share of power is given so that it will

[4] Morris Janowitz (ed.), *Community Political Systems* (New York: The
Free Press of Glencoe, 1961), p. 17.
[5] For political decisions at Springdale, "In no instance is a formula based
on a recognition of conflicting interests which require balancing." (Arthur
Vidich and Joseph Bensman, *Small Town in Mass Society* [Garden City,
N.Y.: Anchor Books, 1960], p. 131.)

not be used. As stated by one mayor, "There's never any difficulty [on the municipal council] once everyone is represented."[6]

The picture reminds one not of Madison, but of Rousseau, and indeed he is a key figure in understanding the rhetoric and practice of French local consensus. The typical French commune is similar to the community that Rousseau delineates in *The Social Contract* and the *Discourse on Political Economy*. The present-day French mayor resembles Rousseau's legislator.

Earlier in this chapter the mayor was compared to a *chef d'orchestre*. The comparison also illuminates the nature of the commune. In the mayor's vision, the commune is much closer to an orchestra than it is, for example, to a marketplace (the image of the polity suggested by Bentham). The two images mayors most frequently use to describe the commune—the family and the business enterprise—and the image of the orchestra all have their source in Rousseau's view of the community, not Madison's, because of what they reveal about the configuration of forces within the commune. In each of the three images, the participants do not compete against each other (as the image of the marketplace suggests). There is a differentiation of tasks, true, but it is for the purpose of better fulfilling the common end. According to the rhetoric of *apolitisme*, harmony necessarily exists among the constituent forces of the commune. It is not a final goal but a constant feature of local life.

Rousseau is helpful in understanding the nature of communal harmony: the rhetoric of *apolitisme* resembles Rousseau's own political vision. Rousseau and the typical French mayor share an appreciation of unanimity.

The more concert reigns in the assemblies, that is, the nearer public opinion approaches unanimity, the greater is the dominance

[6] From an interview with a mayor, "Le Maire, le plus utiles des élus," *Signes du temps*, no. 18 (March 1965), p. 18.

of the general will. On the other hand, long debates, dissensions and tumult proclaim the ascendancy of particular interests and the decline of the State.[7]

Rousseau specifies that the community must be small; the democracy he describes cannot flourish in a large community. Smallness facilitates ease of administration, patriotism, and stability.[8] Both Rousseau and French mayors value smallness because it permits the general will to emerge naturally; unanimity is harder to achieve in a large community, where partial wills are more likely to be expressed and to predominate. Rousseau and Madison are in agreement in believing that partial interests are more likely to emerge, organize, and compete in the large community. Both believed that partial wills result from the development of partial interests and that in the large community partial interests are more numerous and better organized than in the small community. However, whereas Madison felt that the competition of factions best served the public interest, Rousseau believed that the existence of partial interests perverted the general will.[9]

Yet there is a central ambiguity in both Rousseau's and the mayor's vision of the small united community: does the general will emerge by itself? Or is it articulated by someone who thereupon secures its acceptance by the community? Does the general will represent a genuine unanimity of interests among citizens? Or is it a mere artifact of the legislator's craft, skillfully imposed by him on the community?

At first, Rousseau seems to assert that the general will emerges from the communion of like-minded simple people: people need only search their consciences for them to discern

[7] Jean-Jacques Rousseau, "The Social Contract," in Rousseau, *op. cit.,* p. 92.
[8] *Ibid.,* Book II, Chap. ix. However, Rousseau says that the smaller the political community, the less able it is to defend itself.
[9] James Madison, *Federalist Papers,* Nos. 10 and 51. See also McConnell, *op. cit.,* Chap. 4, "The Constituency." Rousseau adds that, if interests are organized, they should be as numerous as possible.

the best public policy. "If, when the people, being furnished with adequate information, held its deliberations, the citizens had no communication with one another, the grand total of the small differences would always give the general will, and the decision would always be good."[1] Rousseau himself, however, soon questions whether this is sufficient when he asks how people are to regulate the conditions of society:

Is it to be by agreement, by a sudden inspiration? . . . How can a blind multitude, which often does not know what it wills, because it rarely knows what is good for it, carry out for itself as great and difficult an enterprise as a system of legislation: . . . This makes the legislator necessary.[2]

Rousseau is discreetly vague about the methods used by the legislator, who cannot "appeal to either force or reason, and [who] must have recourse to an authority of a different order, capable of constraining without violence and persuading without convincing."[3] The role assigned to the legislator indicates that Rousseau does not rely on the people alone, for the legislator must articulate, and get the community to adopt, the general will that it otherwise would not have discerned. If the small community were sufficient unto itself, there would be no need for a legislator. However, in fact, the legislator's task is "an enterprise too difficult for human powers, and, for its execution, [he has] an authority that is no authority."[4]

The dilemma in which the mayor finds himself is that he also must take a central and active part in maintaining communal harmony and consensus, while at the same time claiming that harmony is natural and does not need to be imposed. As with Rousseau's legislator, the French mayor's actual behavior belies his stated position. Local consensus is ambiguous,

[1] Rousseau, *op. cit.*, pp. 25–26.
[2] *Ibid.*, p. 34.
[3] *Ibid.*, p. 37.
[4] *Ibid.* A critical difference between Rousseau's legislator and a French mayor is that the legislator provides a system of laws but does not rule.

for if the natural condition of the commune were unity, mayors would not be forced to exert skillful and patient efforts to prevent opposition from developing. If differences among individuals and groups in the commune were not politically relevant, mayors might not take them into careful consideration. If the commune had common values and interests, mayors might not find it necessary to present their proposals with extreme caution, and would perhaps find it less necessary to consult in advance with those who might otherwise oppose their efforts. If support for the local government was inevitable, in short, mayors would not take such care to guarantee support and to prevent opposition from arising.

The mayor's actions provide a clue to his conception of the community: his obligation is to be active so that he can be nullified. Like the *chef d'orchestre*, he has no instrument to play. He is never heard, yet he holds the most central position; like the *chef d'orchestre*, his effort is expended precisely so that the music will sound natural. It is through his efforts that the music attains its most natural form. The greatest compliment to his talent is for someone listening not to realize that one single human will directs the entire operation and is ultimately responsible for the harmony that the orchestra as a whole creates. He does not work his will through a single instrument; rather, he leads the whole orchestra toward the fulfillment of his vision.

CONCLUSION

The *Practical Guide for the Municipal Orator*, a collection of model speeches for mayors, suggests the following: "Separated by ideas, perhaps, but always united in action, we will promote together the greatest good for our community."[1] Mayors are also supplied with additional advice to share with their municipal councilors:

We must all give our wholehearted support to the communal program. I am confident we will, for I know that each one of us has dedicated himself to protecting the interests entrusted to us. But our concern will be in vain, our efforts quickly nullified, if we give way to partisan passions. . . . If we abandon ourselves to intrigue and to a systematic and sterile controversy, discord and its associated evils will surely result.[2]

French society is not an easy one in which to maintain political stability. In the Third and Fourth Republics, governments succeeded each other every several months. In what might appear difficult circumstances, the French mayor has been unusually successful in divining possibilities for leader-

[1] Pierre-Paul Armand, *Guide pratique de l'orateur municipal* (Paris: Publications Administratives, 1959), p. 10.
[2] *Ibid.*, pp. 3, 7–8.

ship. However, another current in French politics, exemplified by the political styles of both local government and the Fifth Republic, demonstrates that political stability in France is likely to be achieved at a price. In both national and local politics, the establishing of stable political leadership has meant the atrophy of meaningful political debate. Despite mutual animosity, French mayors would not hesitate to agree with their president that a system of governing by political parties is "unstable, uncertain, inconstant."[3]

The authoritarian politics of the Fifth Republic thus becomes more comprehensible viewed against the backdrop of local government. The Fifth Republic's political style is not unknown in France and one need not go back to Louis Napoleon for confirmation. One might speculate that the stability of the Fifth Republic and of local governments is sustained by a congruence in their authority patterns.[4] French local governments and the Fifth Republic also share both an ideology and a practice. The ideology rejects political controversy; the practice is one of paternal leadership by an indispensable man.

If communes are not merely to be "separated by ideas" but are also to be "always united in action," careful thought must be given to how local unity can be ensured. The French mayor plays a decisive role in maintaining communal harmony. In local elections, he forms a broad coalition bringing together members of rival political parties. By giving every group in his commune representation on the dominant list, and thereby on the municipal council, he eliminates the need for groups to sponsor independent lists of their own.

Indeed, one of the municipal council's chief functions is

[3] Press conference of Charles de Gaulle, January 14, 1963, reprinted in *Major Addresses, Statements, and Press Conferences of General Charles de Gaulle: May 19, 1958–January 31, 1964* (New York: French Embassy, n.d.), p. 203.
[4] Harry Eckstein, *A Theory of Stable Democracy* (Research Monograph No. 10; Princeton, N.J., Center of International Studies, 1961).

to give symbolic representation to the commune's vital forces. The council is virtually moribund as the legislative branch of local government and, moreover, is not even expected to play an independent role in communal affairs. A mayor can usually obtain the municipal council's required formal consent without exerting great effort; yet he is careful to secure his councilors' informal approval before officially proposing a project.

In the mayor's view, opposition to his leadership is a betrayal of communal solidarity. Dissidents are criticized for weakening the commune in its struggle with the state. Since the state is regarded as hostile to communal goals, the potential benefits it can provide the commune will not be forthcoming without struggle. Consequently, mayors follow an elaborate procedure to gain state help. Although much of what they do may not be necessary to achieve that goal, their actions nevertheless serve to consolidate their own local position and to maintain unity within their commune.

The mayor believes he is uniquely qualified to discern the commune's interests and to fashion policies which serve those interests. According to the rhetoric of *apolitisme*, the commune is a natural and homogeneous unit; what divides citizens from each other is less important than what unites them. The posture of the French commune toward the outside world is reminiscent of the posture adopted by the French family. And the French mayor is the first to see—and foster—the analogy between himself and the French father.

French local governments provide facilities which materially improve the lives of the commune's residents. A local government offers political stability, comfort, and protection against the outside world. However, the actual value of local governments must be weighed against their potential worth: local governments are predominantly conservative in character.[5]

[5] See Grant McConnell, *Private Power and American Democracy* (New York: Alfred A. Knopf, 1966), especially Chap. 10; and Roscoe C. Martin, *Grass Roots* (University, Ala.: University of Alabama Press, 1957), Chap. III.

Moreover, since potential opposition in most communes is coopted into the ruling oligarchy, there is little chance that citizens will be offered an alternative to the status quo. French local governments mirror an implicit agreement by residents of the commune to exempt local government from the normal processes of democratic politics.

Ironically, French local consensus may facilitate the opposite of what is intended. Because local governments are undemocratic, citizens lose the opportunity of learning how to resolve local problems at the source. Frenchmen may rest content with their local government because they neither ask nor expect it to satisfy their demands. As de Tocqueville observed, citizens may appeal instead for the national government's help to resolve local problems, thereby overburdening the national government and leaving municipal governments less capable of dealing with local needs. The consequence of local consensus may be to invite national intervention in local affairs and thus to increase centralization in France.

In order to evaluate the prevailing practice of French local government, one would need to learn what the consequences would be if municipal politics was more democratic. Is the conservatism of local government related to its undemocratic foundation? What would be the outcome if cleavages over national issues in a commune were reinforced by cleavages over local issues? Might a more democratic political practice burst asunder the bonds that hold the commune together?

French local consensus is ambiguous because it is achieved by excluding significant issues from public consideration and by narrowing the range of local action. Alternatively, if one accepts that—however tenuous—local consensus is an important feature of French municipal life, then local consensus is ambiguous on normative grounds. As with the turbulence of French national politics—although in a quite different way— the consensus prevailing in local politics has hindered the conduct of effective and responsive government in France. Local consensus has deprived Frenchmen of an arena in which to pursue their goals. The structure of French local government has become increasingly outdated, yet municipal leaders generally fail to respond with foresight and vigor. Local governments are relatively inactive in shaping and adapting to changing conditions; as a result, short-run communal unity is achieved to the detriment of long-run viability.

In retrospect, French local consensus may be a product of the apparent exhaustion of ideology in the decades following World War II. Consensus is easier to maintain if expectations and stakes are low. When vital interests are touched, unanimity is likely to decline as people articulate differences instead of concealing them. Local consensus in France has consisted of a negative agreement not to regard local government as an instrument to achieve substantial change. Like the French Third Republic, local governments will probably enjoy unanimous support only so long as demands are few.

Yet such negative consensus is particularly vulnerable. Economic prosperity, better communications, and the rise of what the French call *les forces nouvelles* (new leadership), may all contribute to the development of a more activist outlook and a reduced emphasis on consensus at the local level. Local consensus was made, not born. Although it may decline in the future, as pressures for local action increase, the ambiguous consensus—with its characteristic pattern of ostensible unity existing alongside masked cleavage—persists as a central feature of local government in France.

APPENDIXES

APPENDIX A

A Questionnaire Concerning French Local Politics

❖

I. Des charactéristiques de la commune

1. Combien y a-t-il d'habitants?
2. Quel est le sens du mouvement de la population—accroissement ou diminution?
3. Quels sont les grands problèmes de votre commune? surtout ceux qui vous concernent comme maire?
4. Les finances communales—Quel sorts de problèmes particuliers avez vous?
5. Quels sont les subventions et emprunts de la commune?
6. Est-ce que la commune appartient à des syndicats de commune? Lesquels?

II. La personnalité du maire

1. Depuis quand êtes-vous maire?
2. Demeurez-vous dans la commune dont vous êtes le maire? (Sinon: combien de fois par mois allez-vous dans votre commune?)
3. Est-ce que votre père s'intéressait à l'administration locale? Etait-il un élu?
4. Quelle est votre profession?
5. Combien de temps consacrez-vous à votre mandat?
6. Vous est-il arrivé dans votre profession privée d'éprouver un conflit entre vos fonctions de maire et votre profession privée?

7. Pensez-vous que votre fonction est: l'administration ou la politique?
8. Appartenez-vous à un parti politique? Lequel?
9. Avez-vous d'autres mandats politiques? Lesquels?
10. Avez-vous l'intention de chercher d'autres mandats dans l'avenir?
11. Quels projets avez-vous faits comme maire?
12. Quels sont vos projets nouveaux pour l'avenir?
13. Pourquoi avez-vous voulu devenir maire?
14. Etes-vous content actuellement d'être maire?

III. Des Elections

1. Y a-t-il eu une lutte pour devenir maire?
2. Y avait-il d'autres candidats?
3. Est-ce que la lutte était entre personnalités ou entre partis? (lesquels—locaux ou nationaux?) ou entre les politiques?
4. Quel était votre programme électoral?
5. Pourquoi, vous semble-t-il, avez-vous été élu maire?
6. Quelles sont les qualités indispensables pour être maire?
7. Sont-elles différentes actuellement de ce qu'elles étaient au lendemain de la guerre ou pendant les dernières années? Comment?
8. Est-ce qu'il y a plus d'agitation pour les élections locales que pour les élections législatives? Pourquoi?

IV. Rapports

A. Dans la commune

a. Conseil municipal

1. Combien de réunions du conseil municipal y a-t-il dans l'année?
2. Est-ce que les conseillers municipaux sont actifs, s'intéressent-ils aux problèmes de la commune?
3. Est-ce que le conseil municipal suit votre avis dans la plupart des cas? S'oppose-t-il à vos projets?
4. Donnez-vous votre avis souvent aux conseillers?
5. Etes-vous le chef ou le serviteur du conseil municipal?
6. Y a-t-il des luttes entre le conseil municipal et le maire? dans l'intérieur du conseil municipal?

7. Sur quelle base y a-t-il des divisions dans le conseil municipal? —personnalités, partis politiques, géographiques?
8. Est-ce que le conseil municipal est une institution utile pour la commune? Ou bien pensez-vous qu'il est dépassé et moins utile qu'autrefois?

b. Secrétaire de mairie

1. Est-ce que le secrétaire de mairie fait beaucoup de travail de mairie?
2. Que fait-il comme profession?
3. Combien de fois par semaine vous adressez-vous à lui?

c. Le reste de la commune

1. Quels sont vos rapports avec les chefs de partis? les notabilités? les chefs des groupes, syndicats, cercles, etc.?
2. Quels sont vos rapports avec vos administrés? Viennent-ils souvent à la mairie? chez vous? Vous adressent-ils des demandes? Vous donnent-ils des renseignements? etc.

B. Gouvernement de l'Etat

a. Les hommes politiques

1. Quels sont vos rapports avec les conseillers généraux?
2. Quels sont vos rapports avec votre député?
3. Quels sont vos rapports avec votre sénateur?
4. Quels sont vos rapports avec les autres maires?

b. Le Préfet

1. Combien de fois par mois allez-vous à la préfecture?
2. Vous adressez-vous au préfet ou aux chefs de bureaux ou divisions?
3. Avez-vous des relations personnelles avec les membres de l'administration avec lesquels vous vous trouvez fréquemment en rapport? (préfet, sous-préfet, chefs de bureaux, etc.)
4. Comment sont vos relations avec le préfet? la préfecture? le sous-préfet?
5. Qui connaissez-vous le mieux: le préfet ou le sous-préfet?
6. A qui vous adressez-vous le plus souvent?
7. Lequel préférez-vous?
8. Le préfet et le sous-préfet, essaient-ils de donner leur aide pour que vous puissiez obtenir des subventions?
9. Y a-t-il un moyen politique pour obtenir des subventions?

10. Le préfet ou le sous-préfet, annule-t-il quelquefois des arrêtés du maire ou des déliberations du conseil municipal?

11. Est-ce que le contrôle du préfet est un soutien ou une contrainte pour l'autonomie communale?

12. Est-ce que la tutelle est nécessaire pour les communes? pour légalité, même pour opportunité?

APPENDIX B

The Legal and Financial Powers of French Local Government

※

Article 2 of the Constitution of the Fifth French Republic declares that the sovereignty of the French state is "indivisible" and that it "belongs to the people. . . . No section of the people, nor any individual, may attribute to themselves or himself the exercise thereof." Article 72 names the commune as one of the three basic territorial units of the Republic, along with the departments and the overseas territories. Article 72 continues: "These units shall be free to govern themselves through elected councils and under the conditions stipulated by law." Thus, although French local governments owe their existence to the Constitution, whatever powers they exercise are delegated by the national government. Municipal governments possess no constitutional autonomy beyond the right of mere existence. Decentralization in France occurs at the discretion of the national government; France is a unitary state.

In French administrative law local governments are considered competent, in principle, to decide all matters of local concern. The national legislature, administrative officials, and administrative courts are empowered to determine what specific matters are not of local concern, and in which fields, therefore, local governments may not legislate.

However, once local units are granted autonomous powers, local officials possess legal discretion with regard to the exercise of their official responsibilities. Officials of decentralized units, like local government, are legally independent of the national government.

Several means are used to ensure their legal independence (which, needless to say, may not guarantee independence in fact —as will be discussed below). The selection of local officials helps to guarantee their independence of the national government, for local officials are elected from below rather than appointed from above.

French municipal councils are popularly elected; and the municipal council in a commune elects the commune's mayor. Thus, French local governments are selected by their constituents rather than by the national government.

The independence of local governments is also assured, in legal theory, by their being granted by the national government proper powers which local officials may exercise at their own discretion. Their decisions cannot be modified by national officials, although in certain specified cases communal decisions can be annulled. However, unless the organic law regulating local government is changed, the state possesses only a veto power over local decisions. Municipal officials are not subject to hierarchical control by officials of the national government and, save for exceptions to be reviewed, cannot be issued instructions by the state. The fundamental guarantee of decentralization is that local officials have the right to exercise their legal powers without interference from the state.[1]

The French commune has been given the right of "moral personality" by the state. This right permits local governments to make decisions that are binding upon their constituents. Since France remains a unitary state, however, the granting of powers to local governments remains provisional.

Fictively, the moral personality is an arbitrary creation of the legislator; consequently, he can subordinate it to conditions that please him, limit its rights, and ultimately even destroy it.[2]

As the author of this treatise in administrative law wryly notes, decentralization suffers from a certain "fragility." Nonetheless, the

[1] Georges Vedel, *Droit administratif* (Paris: Presses Universitaires de France, 1961), p. 462; Marcel Waline, *Droit administratif* (Paris: Sirey, 1963), pp. 302–3; and H. Montagnier, "Vingt années d'évolution du régime communal," *Actualités jurisprudence* (April 20, 1966), pp. 204–17. For a general survey of the legal basis of French local government see Brian Chapman, *An Introduction to French Local Government* (London: George Allen & Unwin, 1953).
[2] Georges Burdeau, *Traité de science politique* (Paris: Librairie Générale de Droit et de Jurisprudence, 1949), II, 339.

organic law which specifies the institutions and powers of local government has remained relatively unchanged since it was passed in 1884.

French administrative law makes the important distinction between decentralization and deconcentration. The latter refers to relations among national government officials, all of whom are part of the national administrative hierarchy. Unlike officials of decentralized units, national officials in the provinces, such as prefects, exercise power in the name of the national government. Their decisions are subject to review and revision by their administrative superiors and they can be promoted, rotated, suspended, and issued detailed instructions, just as can any other government bureaucrats. Deconcentration is merely an arrangement for facilitating the exercise of national authority, and the degree of deconcentration is unrelated to the degree of local autonomy.

While the state permits local governments to exercise without impediment the powers granted to them, it retains the right to prevent local officials from committing illegal acts. Local decisions must be formally submitted to a national official who reviews each decision to ensure its legality. Furthermore, because certain local decisions particularly affect the national interest, the national government has specified that in these cases its review power shall extend beyond the determination of mere legality. It has reserved the right to veto these exceptionally important local decisions not only on grounds of illegality but also on the grounds that they are deemed to conflict with the general interest and are unwise on grounds of *policy*.

National officials thus exercise two kinds of veto power over the decisions of local officials. There is a general control over all local governmental decisions so as to ensure their *legality*. In addition, for a small number of important questions, the state reserves the right to review the *wisdom* and the *desirability* of local governmental decisions. (The French call this latter power of review the *tutelle*.)

The classic work on the legal position of local government asserts that communal liberty would be impossible without the *tutelle*.[3] Unless the state can reserve the right to annul certain important local decisions, not because they are *illegal* but because

[3] Roland Maspétiol and Pierre Laroque, *La Tutelle administrative* (Paris: Sirey, 1930), p. 9.

they are *unwise*, there would not be a unitary state but a federal distribution of sovereignty. Rather than the *tutelle* limiting local liberties, Maspétiol and Laroque assert that it makes possible their exercise. They suggest that the *tutelle* is established in the general interest of the state, to guarantee that the liberty granted decentralized authorities will not be misused. More specifically, the *tutelle* protects French citizens against abuses of power by local officials. It safeguards the unity of the state by preventing conflicts between national laws and local decisions; it also ensures that services undertaken by local governments are performed adequately and that there is a minimum of financial waste.

Local Governmental Institutions and Powers

The municipal council together with the mayor comprise the local government. (The powers of subordinate municipal officials —for example, the assistant mayor, town clerk, and town constable—are relatively unimportant and need not be reviewed here.)

The municipal council is the legislative organ of the commune. Its size varies from 9 members in communes with fewer than 100 inhabitants to 37 members in communes with a population of more than 60,000.[4] The municipal council is elected for a six-year term by universal suffrage, and any adult resident or taxpayer in the commune is eligible to run for office.

The electoral law has undergone continual modification; and also varies according to the size of commune. For the 1959 municipal elections, cities of less than 120,000 elected their municipal councils by *scrutin de liste majoritaire à deux tours*: lists of candidates competed, the number of candidates on each list being equal to the number of seats on the municipal council. Candidates who received an absolute majority of votes were elected to the municipal council on the first ballot. If all seats on the municipal council were not filled on the first ballot, a run-off election was held the following week to fill the remaining vacancies; a simple plurality sufficed for election on the second ballot. For the 13 French cities with more than 120,000 (excluding Paris) election was by proportional representation.

[4] France's two largest cities—Marseilles and Lyons—have larger municipal councils. According to decrees of March 1964, Paris is no longer considered a city but has become a unique combination of a commune and a department.

The *scrutin majoritaire* limited the possibility that candidates would be elected from rival lists. Although voters were given the right of *panachage*—they were permitted to vote for candidates from several lists—the probability was that they would vote a straight ticket. Thus, the list that received the largest number of votes would be elected in its entirety, on either the first or the second ballot. A list that received less than a plurality would probably not be represented on the municipal council at all, even if it received a substantial number of votes. In large cities, of course, the use of proportional representation maximized political divisions on the municipal council.

The electoral law was changed in 1964 prior to the 1965 municipal elections, and the *scrutin majoritaire* was extended to even the largest cities. Moreover, in cities of more than 30,000 *panachage* was abolished and coalitions were prohibited on the second ballot among lists that had competed in the first ballot.[5]

By the statute of 1884 on local governmental organization, the municipal council is granted power "to regulate all communal affairs by its deliberations."[6] This basic delegation of responsibility to the municipal council remains in force and establishes the principle that the municipal council is competent to legislate, unless a law or an administrative court ruling explicitly declares the contrary. Local governments are legally free to do whatever is not explicitly forbidden to them by law. Because the decisions of the municipal council are self-regulatory, its specific powers are not enumerated in French administrative law. Local governmental powers can be divided into four categories: (1) decisions that can be made with merely routine state approval so as to ensure legality; (2) decisions that require additional state approval on grounds of wisdom and desirability (the *tutelle*); (3) decisions that local governments are forbidden to make; and (4) mandatory decisions that local officials must make pursuant to

<hr>

[5] The new law was reported to be designed to maximize UNR strength by polarizing political parties between the Communist Party and the UNR. It was also said the law was designed to weaken Gaston Defferre's chances of retaining his mayor's position in Marseilles. On both counts the law failed. See Edmond Taylor, "French Politics at the Municipal Level," *The Reporter* (April 8, 1965), pp. 31–32. Also see the election results in Table 7 of Chapter VII.

[6] Article 61, Law of April 5, 1884. Consult here Pierre Bouffard, *Le Contrôle des délibérations du conseil municipal* (Paris: Publications Administratives, 1957).

carrying out their duties as required by law. Actions falling into categories 2–4 are specified in French administrative law. But there is no enumeration of the areas ([1] above) in which local governments are free to legislate, for they are presumed competent in principle unless a law explicitly limits their liberty.

Before taking effect, all local decisions must be approved by state officials, who judge whether the decision is legally proper. Administrative law specifies that municipal council deliberations are to be automatically nullified if they violate a national law or an administrative court ruling; if they are directed to matters beyond the competence of the municipal council—that is, if they do not relate to communal affairs; or if they are not passed at a legal meeting of the municipal council ([3] above). The municipal council is also forbidden to publish proclamations or to state partisan preferences.[7]

After the municipal council passes a deliberation, a copy is sent to the national official who is authorized to review the deliberation—in most cases the subprefect of the *arrondissement* in which the commune is located. Approval of a deliberation is considered to have been granted unless the deliberation is explicitly annulled within fifteen days after the date of its receipt at the subprefecture.

Certain decisions made by local governments are considered to be of particular importance. In these exceptional cases, which are specified by law, the state reserves the right to veto the local decision and to prevent it from taking effect even if it does not violate a law but is simply imprudent ([2] above). Grounds for disapproval thus go beyond the criterion of legality.

In order to limit harassment by the national government, local decisions whose wisdom can be reviewed by national officials must be explicitly enumerated in administrative law. Although the number of decisions in this category has been reduced in recent years, the *tutelle* still remains important in legal theory. For all communes, approval is required for decisions to undertake new municipal facilities, decisions affecting the communal patrimony, the naming of streets after living persons or historical figures, the levying of certain taxes, and regulations concerning municipal

---

[7] France, *Code Municipal* (1957), Article 42. Article 43 specifies other grounds on which a municipal council deliberation may be annulled if the prefect so chooses, for example, if a municipal councilor had a financial interest in the outcome of a council vote.

employees. Small communes are subject to additional restrictions. In communes under 9,000, the wisdom of the local budget and loans undertaken by the commune must also be approved; in communes over 9,000 this approval is required only in unusual cases.[8] After deliberations subject to a national review on grounds of prudence are voted by the municipal council, they are sent to the relevant authority, usually the subprefect, for approval; if not explicitly rejected within forty days from date of receipt, they are considered approved.[9]

The municipal council is also required by law to take certain actions which are deemed to be in the general interest. It must give advice upon specified matters when asked by state officials— for example, classifying local roads, creating bureaus of social aid, and urban planning. It must produce a balanced budget and review the financial accounts presented by the mayor. It is required to provide funds to meet obligatory expenses, including upkeep of the town hall and communal archives, provision for fire prevention service, salaries of local police, the salary of school teachers and maintenance of schools, expenses for hygiene and social aid, and repayment of local government debts ([4] above).

If these obligatory functions are not performed, the prefect possesses exceptional powers over local governments. After warning a recalcitrant local government, he may then "substitute for office"—that is, he may perform the required action in the name of the commune. The conditions under which this right of substitution can be exercised are precisely defined: the municipal council must first be notified of its error; it is only after this warning goes unheeded that the prefect can use the more extreme powers. Even then the prefect must do no more in the commune's name than remedy the violation—for example, a prefect can raise taxes or lower expenditures to balance a commune's budget, but he cannot lower taxes if he considers them imprudently high, nor can he increase expenditures unless the municipal council has failed to provide funds for a mandatory expenditure.

Local governments are legally free to undertake an enormous

[8] If the interest on loans exceeds 10 per cent of the *recettes ordinaires* or the local tax rate exceeds a figure set by the Conseil d'Etat. (France, *Code Municipal*, 1957, Article 48.)
[9] The system of tacit approval is opposed vehemently by Maspétiol and Laroque for, in their opinion, it blurs the national government's responsibility to judge the prudence of these important local decisions. (Maspétiol and Laroque, *op. cit.*, pp. 346-64.)

number of activities. The most usual local responsibilities include the routine upkeep of roads, schools, and other public buildings. But if they choose, local governments may give financial grants-in-aid to voluntary associations in the commune. They may also supply running water to inhabitants and build public baths, parks, monuments, housing, sporting fields, nurseries, libraries, and industrial parks. These are but a few significant examples of the great range of possibilities for communal action available to local governments.[1]

Whatever centralization prevails in France is not merely a result of legal servitude. Local governments in the United States are in no more enviable a situation vis-à-vis state governments than are French local governments toward the national government. In effect, all French communes—from the smallest to the largest —are automatically granted the American equivalent of home rule.

The mayor is the commune's chief executive and its most important official. After a municipal council has been elected, its first act is to elect a mayor from its ranks. Any municipal councilor is eligible to become mayor, and his six-year term as mayor coincides with that of the municipal council who elected him. The municipal council also elects at least one assistant mayor from among its ranks; he has no independent legal powers, and the duties he performs are delegated to him by the mayor. Mayors are prohibited by law from receiving salaries; for fulfilling their duties, they are only paid a small indemnity, which is in fact less than the expenses they incur.[2]

The mayor acts in three different legal capacities.[3] His relation to the municipal council and to the state varies according to the

[1] See also Maurice Fretin, "L'Autonomie et la tutelle communale" (unpublished thesis, University of Paris, Faculty of Law, 1951); Jean Singer, "L'Interventionnisme communal," *Revue administrative,* XI (November–December 1958), 647–48; and Lucien Valentin, *L'Action administrative dans la vie rurale* (Paris: Berger-Levrault, 1961).

[2] The indemnity varies according to the size of commune and is related to the salary schedule of the national civil service. In tiny communes, a mayor's indemnity is several hundred dollars a year; in the largest cities of Marseilles and Lyons, about $4,000.

[3] See Jean Rivero, "Le Maire, exécuteur des délibérations du conseil municipal," *Revue critique de législation et de jurisprudence,* LVII (July–October 1937), 535–605; Schmitt, *op. cit.*; and Dominique Tafani, "Le Statut personnel du maire" (unpublished thesis, University of Paris, Faculty of Law, 1958).

capacity in which he is acting. The mayor is the representative of the state in the commune. Within the commune his role is analogous to that of the prefect in the department and, when acting as the state's agent in the commune, the national government may delegate duties to the mayor. In the words of the *Code Municipal*, he performs these powers "under the authority of the national administration."[4]

The tasks that mayors and their subordinates perform as state representatives are mainly routine and clerical. The mayor is required, for example, to publish (and he may be asked to enforce) national laws or court decisions. Under the mayor's direction municipal employees keep the civil register of births, deaths, and marriages. The mayor is charged with establishing the electoral list of the commune's eligible voters and the draft roll of those eligible for military service. The mayor can be delegated other duties by the state, usually also of a routine nature.[5]

In his performance of national responsibilities the mayor is considered to be part of the national administrative apparatus. For these "primarily administrative functions . . . he acts exactly like a state bureaucrat. . . ."[6] He can be issued detailed instructions by national officials and they can revise or reject his decisions at their discretion. The mayor is the only agent of the state in most communes. When discharging his responsibilities as state representative, the municipal council cannot control the mayor's performance.

The mayor's second role is that of president and agent of the municipal council. Article 75 of the *Code Municipal* enumerates the responsibilities that the mayor performs "under the control of the municipal council and the surveillance of the national administration." (By contrast, when he is acting as an agent of the state, the mayor is not under national *surveillance* but under national *authority*.) The mayor's powers as agent of the municipal council include the major executive tasks of local government: conserving and administering the property of the commune, preparing and proposing the municipal budget, ordering payments

---

[4] France, *Code Municipal*, 1957, Article 77.
[5] Some authors consider the mayor to be overburdened by the tasks he performs for the state. See René Savatier, "La Crise et l'avenir des maires rurales," *Etudes* (March 1948), p. 330; and Charles Schmitt, *Le Maire de la commune rurale* (Paris: Berger-Levrault, 1959), pp. 27–29.
[6] Tafani, *op. cit.*, p. 2.

authorized by the budget, directing communal projects, negotiating contracts voted by the municipal council, and executing municipal council decisions.[7]

The municipal council cannot impeach the mayor on its own authority if he fails to perform the tasks that he has been delegated. However, the municipal council can appeal to the national government and a mayor who has failed to fulfill his legal duties can thereupon be suspended or dismissed from office by the state. (Such outright conflicts are rare since the mayor is elected by the municipal council and, in addition, exercises a great deal of informal influence.)

The mayor also acts as the executive of the commune and possesses powers which enable him to exercise this responsibility. As the commune's executive, the mayor acts independently of the municipal council and the state, although the state retains a right of review to ensure legality.

Article 64 of the Code Municipal charges the mayor with the sole direction of communal administration. He is the hierarchical superior of all municipal employees and has the power to name, promote, and dismiss them.[8]

In his capacity as chief executive of the commune, the mayor also possesses the municipal police power.[9] Article 97 of the Code Municipal states: "The object of the municipal police power is to assure good order, safety, security and public health." The mayor is authorized to issue decrees to achieve these aims which become valid one month after their deposit at the prefecture or subprefecture.[1] Within the broad jurisdiction of the municipal police power, specific subjects of regulation include: traffic regulation, and otherwise assuring safety and free passage in streets and public places; prevention of attacks on the public health and

[7] See Rivero's excellent article on this aspect of a mayor's duties. Loc. cit.
[8] However, a law passed in April 1952, and incorporated in the Code Municipal, 1957, Articles 477–626, instituted rigorous state supervision of the conditions of municipal employment. The law thereby limited a mayor's powers over communal employees.
[9] For further discussions of the mayor's police powers, see Maurice Daniel, Les Pouvoirs de police des maires (Paris: Librarie Technique, 1960); Jean Singer, Le Maire et ses pouvoirs de police (Paris: Berger-Levrault, 1959); and "Les Pouvoirs de police des maires," a special issue of Etude des problèmes municipaux, no. 10 (June 1966).
[1] Controversy exists whether state control can extend to the wisdom of a decree as well as its legality. See Schmitt, op. cit., p. 25, who denies that it can; and Maspétiol and Laroque, op. cit., pp. 200 ff., who assert that state control extends to prudence.

tranquillity; and ordering repair or demolition of buildings in dangerous condition. An enormous variety of measures is permissible within each area. For example, the Conseil d'Etat has held that a mayor can censor films shown in his commune (or prohibit their being shown) if he decides that they constitute a menace to public safety, prohibit sky-writing in the airspace over his commune, and prevent clocks from striking the hour too loudly!

Mayors are given broad legal powers. Either as agent of the municipal council and particularly as the commune's chief executive, a mayor may effect substantial changes in his commune.

However, legal competence is not sufficient to ensure actual independence. Local finances are another important factor to be considered.

Local Finances

Local governments have increasingly been subject to financial hardship as local investments are undertaken without adequate tax revenues available. Local expenditures rose from 10 billion francs in 1958 to nearly 15 billion francs in 1962. Municipal revenue comes from four major sources.[2] One of the two largest sources of income for communes is derived from a retail sales tax of about 2.6 per cent on all products sold in France. The national government collects the tax and returns more than half to the local government in the commune where the purchase was made. About one-quarter is given to the departmental general councils; the remainder is deposited in a national equalization fund and redistributed annually to all local governments on the basis of the commune's population. The purpose of the fund is to ensure that all communes will benefit from the sales tax—not merely those communes in which there is a large volume of retail sales. In 1962 income from the sales tax accounted for 22 per cent of communal receipts.[3]

The *centimes* are the other largest source of communal revenue.

[2] Jean Cathlineau, *Le Contrôle des finances communales en France* (Paris: Librairie Générale de Droit et du Jurisprudence, 1963); Robert Lainville, *Le Budget communal*, 8th ed. (Paris: Sirey, 1959); and "Les Finances communales," special issue of *Etude des problèmes municipaux*, no. 7 (September 1965).

[3] "Les Finances communales," *ibid.*, pp. 19, 65. The local tax structure is in the process of being reformed. See Jean-Pierre Dussaife, "Le Parlement face à la réforme de taxe sur le chiffre d'affaires," *Revue française de science politique*, XVI (June 1966), 521–31.

The *centime* is a tax on real estate, developed property, and wealth as well as on the professions and business. Its name stems from the fact that it was once 1/100 of a national tax. However, although the national tax was abolished half a century ago, the fictional base continues to be used to calculate the *centime*. The rate of the *centime* is set by each local government, within ceilings established by the national government. Since a local government must set the tax rate high enough to balance its budget, the tax actually set reflects the goals that the local government hopes to achieve. Unlike the local sales tax, the rate of the *centime* can be regulated by a local government to yield a given amount of revenue. In relation to the receipts of all local governments, the *centime* also represented about 22 per cent of a commune's receipts in 1956.[4]

As communal investments increase, direct taxes (the *centime*) have accounted for an increasing proportion of local receipts, indirect taxes (the local sales tax) for a diminishing proportion. Whereas in 1956 the local sales tax yielded nearly twice the revenue produced by the *centime*, the two taxes yielded the same amount of revenue in 1964. As communes are subjected to rising financial burdens, local tax rates have had to be raised accordingly.

Another important source of funds for local governments is provided by loans used to finance public works.[5] While local governments have the right to borrow from private banks, longer term loans at lower interest can be obtained from government banks and government investment funds. Over three-quarters of the loans to communes are provided by one source, the Caisse des Dépôts et Consignations, the government savings bank.[6] However, before the commune can receive a loan from a government bank, the project which the loan will finance must be declared eligible to receive a loan by the commune's prefect. The effect of government-provided loans is to centralize further France's administrative system.

Communes are resorting to loans at a rapidly increasing extent. (Of course the commune must raise sufficient funds, either through income from the local retail tax or from the *centime*,

---

[4] "Les Finances communales," *ibid.*
[5] André de Laubadère, "Les Emprunts des collectivités locales en France," *International Review of Administrative Sciences*, XXVIII (1962), 1–8.
[6] François Bloch-Lainé, "Caisse des dépôts et consignations," in "Demain . . . les communes," *Regards sur la France*, IX (July 1965), 151–52.

to amortize the loan.) In 1962 loans accounted for 19 per cent of local governmental receipts.[7]

A far smaller source of local revenue comes from national grants-in-aid to help finance local investments; such *subventions* represented about 7 per cent of communal receipts in 1962.[8] These grants-in-aid are "a means used by the state to stimulate and control municipal services."[9] Grants-in-aid are given to the local government by a national ministry for specific purposes—for example, to construct a municipal hospital—the grant varying in amount according to the cost of the project and in percentage according to the type of project undertaken.[1] Some projects are undertaken by a commune nearly entirely at state expense—for example, public water facilities; other projects, such as sporting fields, must be built with only minimal state support. According to one observer, "There are as many procedures to obtain government grants as there are sources of grants within the government."[2] Although the advent of national and regional planning has produced some order, procedures by which the state accords grants remain cumbersome, complicated, and irrational.

Despite the relatively small amounts of state grants, they play an extraordinarily important role in a commune's life since state grants are used to finance local investments. Nearly two-thirds of local governmental expenditures are used to meet current expenses —salaries of municipal employees, road maintenance, and repair of public buildings; and the revenue available for investments is therefore limited. Since state financial help is used mainly for new projects that a commune undertakes, *subventions* assume an importance far out of proportion to their actual amount. Most local projects probably could not be undertaken without the state's financial participation.

Most writers agree that the ample legal powers local govern-

[7] "Les Finances communales," *op. cit.*, p. 19. On May 4, 1966, the government created the Caisse de l'Aide à l'Equipement des Collectivités Locales to provide loans to communes.
[8] *Ibid.*
[9] Lainville, *op. cit.*, p. 166; also see Jean Boulouis, *Essai sur la politique des subventions administratives* (Paris: Armand Colin, 1951).
[1] See *Financement des travaux d'équipement des collectivités locales* (Paris: Caisse des Dépôts et Consignations, 1962), and "Les Subventions de l'état aux communes" (Mimeographed instruction, Service d'Information des Maires, n.d.).
[2] See the discussion by Paul Guerrier, in *Départements et Communes* (September–October 1963), pp. 289–300.

ments enjoy are more than balanced by their financial dependence. Whereas local governments are legally free to undertake local improvements, it is rare that a commune can finance improvements from its own sources of revenue. The local tax base is extremely limited and few communes derive enough income from other sources to be economically self-sufficient. In 1962 only about one-fifth of local investments were financed directly from local tax revenues. Over one-half the funds for local investments came from loans; the remainder from state grants.[3]

Nonetheless, local expenditures play an important part in the French economy. Local expenditures have represented between 25 and 30 per cent of total government expenditures for non-military purposes in recent years. Local and national government expenditures vary at about the same rate and both are increasing at about 11 per cent each year.[4]

Granted that financial servitude severely limits the possibilities open to French local governments, local governments in the United States and Great Britain are also hindered by insufficient funds.[5] Despite limitations, French local governments are relatively free—legally and financially—to pursue their goals.

[3] "Les Finances communales," *op. cit.*, p. 23.
[4] *Ibid.*, p. 12. General council expenditures are included with local expenditures in these figures; however, they represent a small proportion of local expenditures.
[5] Brian Chapman concludes that French local governments are somewhat less autonomous but more vital than English local governments. (*Op. cit.*, p. 221.)

APPENDIX C

Professions de Foi
and Lists of Candidates from
Two Communes of the Gironde

ÉLECTIONS MUNICIPALES DU
8 MARS 1959
COMMUNE DE GRADIGNAN

❖

Liste de Concentration Républicaine
et d'Intérêts Communaux

Chères Concitoyennes, Chers Concitoyens,

Le 8 mars vous devrez choisir un Conseil Municipal. **De votre choix dépendra,** tant au point de vue matériel que moral, **l'évolution de notre commune** au cours des six années qui vont suivre.

Vos élus devront œuvrer avec un esprit de large compréhension et de progrès dans le respect de la tradition.

Le Maire et ses Conseillers sortants ont conscience d'avoir **servi avec loyauté et efficacité** les intérêts de la commune et l'expérience qu'ils ont acquise dans l'exercice de leurs fonctions leur donne le droit de solliciter avec confiance le renouvellement de leur mandat.

Avant de vous parler de l'avenir, ils tiennent à vous exposer comment **ils ont respecté les engagements qu'ils avaient pris en 1953.**

Jugez-en vous-même:

POUR LA VOIRIE, nous avions promis: Le classement dans la voirie départementale d'un chemin reliant le bourg de Gradignan à Villenave-d'Ornon.

Non seulement nous l'avons obtenu, mais également celui du Chemin V.O. 3 nous reliant à Pessac, soit en tout 5 km. 600.

Rappelez-vous l'état lamentable de nos routes. A ce jour, plus de 21 kilomètres de chemins vicinaux ont été goudronnés, tout en assurant l'entretien des 40 autres kilomètres.

De nombreuses routes ont été redressées, élargies (chemin de la Course, chemin du Solarium, chemin de la Voie Romaine à Caillou avec son rond-point de la Poterie, chemin de Ripotte à la Fontaine de Monjous).

Du pont d'Ornon, effondré et interdit à la circulation pendant un an, nous avons fait un pont d'avenir à deux voies charretières.

Pour l'ADDUCTION D'EAU, nous avions promis l'établissement d'un projet.

Aujourd'hui, malgré les difficultés financières, 43 millions de travaux ont été effectués.

POUR LES ECOLES, nous avions promis l'exécution d'un projet de groupe scolaire.

Ce groupe est réalisé, avec 28 classes, sa cuisine pouvant servir 1.000 repas et son réfectoire. Cet ensemble, équipé de matériel neuf, compte parmi les mieux adaptés de l'agglomération bordelaise.

Sur le PLAN ECONOMIQUE ET SOCIAL, nous avions promis de favoriser, dans toute la mesure du possible la construction de maisons d'habitation.

L'équipement en eau et en gaz, la garantie d'emprunt donnée à Baticoop et le projet d'assainissement ont facilité l'édification de près de 250 logements.

A la Mairie, un service spécialisé est chargé de la constitution des dossiers pour les économiquement faibles.

Livres et fournitures scolaires sont distribués gratuitement aux élèves depuis 1954.

La consultation des nourrissons est assurée toutes les semaines depuis 1953.

Poul l'ASSAINISSEMENT nous avions promis l'établissement d'un projet.

A l'heure actuelle, 36 millions de travaux ont été effectués, comprenant 5 kilomètres de canalisation et une station d'épuration d'eaux usées.

En outre, nous avons fait canaliser les eaux pluviales le long de nombreuses voies (le Courneau, Branne, Bénédigues, Martinon, etc.).

Nous avons multiplié et étendu à l'ensemble de la commune le service d'enlèvement des ordures ménagères.

POUR L'ELECTRIFICATION, nous avions promis l'exécution d'un projet de renforcement et d'extension du réseau.

23 millions ont été utilisés à cet effet.

En outre, 32 projecteurs fluorescents ont été mis en place à Beausoleil et dans la traversée du bourg.

L'éclairage public a été quintuplé dans l'ensemble de la commune.

Pour les **ZONES DE SALAIRE, nous avions promis** de tout faire pour obtenir la modification de la loi sur les zones de salaires.

Ce problème, vital pour notre commune, va bientôt être résolu.

Dans le **DOMAINE SPORTIF, nous avions promis** un projet complet de stade et de bain-douche.

La compression du budget de l'Education nationale ne nous a pas permis sa réalisation.

Toutefois, de confortables **vestiaires et des douches ont été mis à la disposition des sportifs.**

Notre activité, loin de se borner à ces réalisations, et malgré les difficultés financières, a permis de procéder à:

— La construction et l'aménagement de 15 logements d'instituteurs.

— La création d'un fonds de chômage.

— La remise en état du cimetière.

— L'achat et l'aménagement de la place de Beausoleil avec report du terminus.

— L'achat d'une benne-tasseuse.

Mais, comment avon-nous pu réaliser tout cela?

Nous avons sollicité et obtenu **167 millions 500.000 fr.** de subventions contre **158.240 fr.** de 1947 à 1952.

Nous avons sollicité et obtenu **116 millions** d'emprunt contre **1.720.000 fr.** de 1947 à 1952.

Soit, au total **283 millions 500.000 francs d'investissements,** sans faire supporter aux contribuables une charge excessive.

Voilà pour le passé,

Voici pour l'avenir:

Sans préjuger des moyens dont nous disposerons, nous voulons, dans tous les domaines, continuer et amplifier l'œuvre commencée, et nous entendons poursuivre l'action déjà engagée, en faveur de la famille, de la jeunesse, des vieillards, du logement, etc. ...

Notre action portera plus spécialement sur:
— L'adduction d'eau pour l'ensemble de la commune;
— L'amélioration du réseau routier par le goudronnage généralisé;
— L'extension et le renforcement de l'électrification et d'intensification de l'éclairage public;
— La mise en service de nouveaux intinéraires d'autobus (Colinat, Ornon, Bénédigues, Monjons).
— L'extension du réseau d'eaux usées et la création d'un réseau de canalisations d'eaux pluviales;
— La pose de bordures, caniveaux, trottoirs;
— L'extension et l'amélioration du Service social communal;
— La poursuite de l'aménagement de la place de l'Eglise, avec suppression de l'îlôt insalubre;
— L'aide au logement;
— L'extension des canalisations du gaz de Lacq;
— L'aménagement du parc de la Mairie.

D'autres problèmes réclament aussi une solution:
— La construction d'un nouveau groupe scolaire, avec création d'un Cours complémentaire et d'écoles maternelles dans les quartiers;
— L'aménagement complet d'un Stade avec piscine;
— L'achat à l'Etat de la propriété du Solarium et son utilisation à des fins sociales;
— La création d'un Foyer Municipal avec bibliothèque et salle de jeu;
— L'abbattement pour charges de familles sur les impositions mobilières.

Le Maire et ses Conseillers sortants ont tenu à s'adjoindre des hommes qui, à des titres divers, ont fait preuve de dévouement à la chose publique et sont donc représentatifs de la population gradignanaise.

Tous ensemble, animés de cet esprit de large compréhension et de progrès, nous sommes décidés à œuvrer toujours dans le sens du mieux-être.

Electrices, Electeurs!

Nous faisons appel à votre sagesse, à votre clairvoyance.

Il ne dépend que de vous que se poursuive l'essor donné à notre petite Patrie.

Votez toutes et tous pour la liste ROUMEGOUX toute entière.

Vive la République! Vive Gradignan! Vive la France!

Vu, les Candidats.

❖❖❖

ÉLECTIONS MUNICIPALES
DU 8 MARS 1959
COMMUNE DE GRADIGNAN

❖

Liste de Concentration Républicaine
et d'Intérêts Communaux

ROUMEGOUX Bernard, Maire sortant, Commerçant.

FAURE Mary, Adjoint au Maire, Propriétaire.

BOULINEAU Robert-Jean, Dessinateur industriel, Conseiller sortant.

BOURDONCLE Blanche-Emilienne, Pharmacien, Conseiller sortant.

COMMAGERE Maurice, Artisan tonnelier, Conseiller sortant.

DUMESTRE André-Victor, Commerçant, Conseiller sortant.

FOURNIER Henri-Pierre, Conducteur de travaux.

GAUTIER Marcel, Rédacteur. C. A. F.

GLANNES Odette, Propriétaire, Conseiller sortant.

GOBEAU Jean, Commerçant.

HELIOT Jean, Agent Commercial.

HOUQUES René, Entreprise de Transports, Conseiller sortant.

LABORDE Roger-Louis, Ingénieur, Conseiller sortant.

LAGRANGE René, Agent technique P.T.T.

LASSALLE-CARRERE Gustave-Pierre, Propriétaire, Conseiller sortant.

LASSAUTONIE Raymond, Commerçant.

LATRILLE Robert, Dessinateur.

LEGER René, Préparateur en Pharmacie, Conseiller sortant.

LE LANN Jean, Représentant de Commerce, Conseiller sortant.

LESTAGE Arnaud, Pensionné de guerre.

PAPILLON Jean-Gaston, Représentant de commerce.

PETIT Claude, Professeur d'horticulture en retraite, Conseiller sortant.

TAILLEUR Robert, Employé de Commerce.

Vu: Les Candidats.

COMMUNE DE PODENSAC
ÉLECTIONS MUNICIPALES
DU 8 MARS 1959

Liste d'Union

pour la Défense des Intérêts Communaux

PRÉSENTÉE PAR

Jacques Lillet

MAIRE SORTANT

Chers Concitoyens,

Nous arrivons au terme du mandat que vous avez bien voulu nous confier pour administrer notre commune voici bientôt six ans. Nous nous sommes efforcés de justifier votre confiance en travaillant sans bruit, pour le bien commun, avec le plus total dévouement.

Il nous a fallu aplanir bien des difficultés, résoudre des problèmes urgents et y apporter des solutions rationnelles en limitant au minimum l'effort des contribuables.

Nous avons défendu avec vigueur les intérêts de notre collectivité locale sur le plan départemental. Mais les problèmes économiques et sociaux ont retenu toute notre attention et nous avons pensé qu'il était de notre devoir de jeter un cri d'alarme aux responsables nationaux de notre région pour le sort réservé à nos campagnes rurales trop longtemps délaissées au profit illusoire et factice des concentrations urbaines provinciales qui constituent la même erreur que l'hypertrophie congestive de Paris et de la Région Parisienne.

Nous n'avons aucune prétention, si ce n'a celle d'avoir rempli notre mission avec courage et probité en continuant l'œuvre de nos prédécesseurs et en préparant l'avenir.

Le bilan de ces six années d'administration est nettement positif, non seulement par l'équilibre des finances communales, mais aussi par les travaux et les réalisations que vous avez pu constater.

PRINCIPALES AMÉLIORATIONS RÉALISÉES

RECHARGEMENT ET REVETEMENT CHAUSSEES:
Vicinal nº 2 de Brouquet à la limite d'Illats.
— nº 5 de Cérons.
— nº 9 des Tuilières.
— nº 11 du cimetière aux Cabanes.
— nº 14 du Mayne d'Imbert.
— nº 16 des Cabanes à la route nationale.
Longueur ensemble: 4 km 800.

AMENAGEMENT DE LA PLACE DE L'EGLISE
Avec élargissement du chemin vicinal permettant à tout véhicules d'utiliser le chemin de ceinture du bourg de Podensac.

AMELIORATION DU CHEMIN VICINAL Nº 13
Dans le quartier des Fontaines.

ASSAINISSEMENT DE VOIES URBAINES
Rue Général-Saint-Marc.
Rue Venizelos.
Rue Gagne-Petit.

Ruelle reliant la place Gambetta à la Grande-Rue.

Impasse aboutissant rue d'Angleterre et desservant dix immeubles.

Impasse attenante à la voie ferrée en prolongement du chemin départemental 117.

REFECTION DE LA CHAUSSEE DE LA RUE SABIN-DARLAN

ASSAINISSEMENT CARREFOUR DES RUES GENERAL SAINT-MARC et SABIN-DARLAN avec canalisation des eaux usées dans le fossé bordant le «Sporting».

CREATION DES LOTISSEMENTS DU CHATEAU D'EAU et des TUILIERES

Avec améliorations sensibles, de voirie (non terminées), le terrain aménagé étant cédé aux intéressés à très bas prix.

AMENAGEMENT COQUET DU JARDIN DE LA MAIRIE

CONSTRUCTION DE W.-C. PUBLICS ET D'UN ABRI POUR LES VOYAGEURS EMPRUNTANT L'AUTOBUS avec aménagement de points de stationnement pour les autobus.

REMISE EN ETAT DE LA HALLE ET ABATTAGE DES ORMES

CONSTRUCTION D'UNE CLASSE SUPPLEMENTAIRE ET D'UN PREAU A L'ECOLE DES FILLES

Semblable amélioration est prévue côté garçons. Revêtement des cours des écoles. Gratuité des fournitures scolaires.

ECIMAGE DES ARBRES DU FOIRAIL

Travail qui s'imposait pour des motifs de sécurité et d'hygiene.

REGULARISATION DU PROFIL DES ALLEES DU PORT

RENOUVELLEMENT DE LA PLANTATION DE PEUPLIERS EN BORDURE DU CHENAL

EXTENSION DU RESEAU DE DISTRIBUTION D'EAU POTABLE aux écarts.

RENFORCEMENT ET EXTENSION DU RESEAU DE DISTRIBUTION D'ENERGIE ELECTRIQUE

AMELIORATIONS AU TERRAIN DE SPORT (entrée et clôture terrain football—Aménagement du terrain de basket).

SIRENE INCENDIE

AMELIORATIONS ROUTE D'ILLATS

ENTRETIEN DES BATIMENTS COMMUNAUX: toiture ancienne mairie—Bains-Douches.

REORGANISATION DE LA POLICE DE LA FOIRE SAINTE-CATHERINE

PROJETS A L'ÉTUDE

Nouveau lotissement dans l'enclos Gans.
Piscine dans le Parc Municipal du Château Chavat.
Aménagements au terrain de sports.
Création d'un terrain de camping.
Aménagement cour de la gare.
Eclairage public.
Réfection de la pouponnière.

On a défini la commune comme «l'association des habitants d'une agglomération en vue de s'administrer, de se défendre, de pourvoir à la satisfaction des besoins matériels et moraux que fait naître le voisinage».

C'est dans l'esprit de cette définition que nous sommes appliqués à maintenir la personnalité harmonieuse de notre petite cité, à améliorer son caractére accueillant, à venir en aide aux déshérités et à faciliter la tâche de tous dans la mesure de nos possibilités mais toujours avec la meilleure volonté.

Nous avons été les témoins de vos joies et de vos peines pendant ces six années qui comptent pour les hommes mais qui entrent à peine en ligne de compte pour la vie d'une collectivité locale comme la nôtre qui prend son essor et pour l'équipement de laquelle il reste beaucoup à faire.

Le temps est en effet un facteur essentiel pour la réalisation des aménagements nécessaires à notre Commune si l'on veut équilibrer ses charges de toute nature avec ses possibilités financières limitées.

Si notre administration et notre gestion vous ont donné satisfaction, nous nous permettons de solliciter le renouvellement de notre mandat pour continuer ce que nous avons commencé.

Nous nous présentons à vos suffrages avec équipe en partie renouvelée du fait du décès de notre regretté collègue Pierre VINCENT et de plusieurs Conseillers municipaux démissionnaires ou qui ont tenu à ne pas se représenter.

L'administration d'une commune est pour nous un service civique. Vous nous avez vus à l'œuvre et désormais vous pouvez mieux nous juger.

Confiants dans votre verdict, comme il sied à des hommes libres avant conscience du devoir accompli, nous vous demandons de voter tous, liste entière, sans panachage, le dimanche 8 mars 1959 pour:

LILLET Jacques — BIOT Gilbert — CHASSAIGNE Raymond
CLAVERIE Marcel — DUPONT Marcel — EXPERT
Valmont — FONTEYREAUD Marcel — FURT Henri
ISTILART Martin — JEAN Yves — LAFFARGUE
Georges — LEVEQUE Henri — MAUGEIN Antoine
PAULY Paul — PENDANX René — RIVIERE Pierre
STERLIN Edouard:

VIVE PODENSAC!

VIVE LA FRANCE!

VIVE LA RÈPUBLIQUE!

COMMUNE DE PODENSAC
ÉLECTIONS MUNICIPALES
DU 8 MARS 1959

Liste d'Union
pour la Défense des Intérêts Communaux
PRÉSENTÉE PAR

Jacques Lillet
CONSEILLER GÉNÉRAL

LILLET Jacques, Avocat à la Cour, maire sortant.
BIOT Gilbert, Employé de l'Hospice.
CHASSAIGNE Raymond, Motoculteur, Conseiller sortant.
CLAVERIE Marcel, Artisan.
DUPONT Marcel, Viticulteur, Conseiller sortant.
EXPERT Valmont, Agent d'assurance.

FONTEYREAUD Marcel, Retraité de la S.N.C.F.

FURT Henri, Cheminot, Conseiller sortant.

ISTILART Martin, Comptable, Conseiller sortant.

JEAN Yves, Artisan, Conseiller sortant.

LAFFARGUE Georges, Retraité, Médaillé militaire, Conseiller sortant.

LEVEQUE Henri, Courtier en vins.

MAUGEIN Antoine, Viticulteur.

PAULY Paul, Notaire.

PENDANX René, Ouvrier boulanger, Conseiller sortant.

RIVIERE Pierre, Artisan, Conseiller sortant.

STERLIN Edouard, Viticulteur.

Vu: LES CANDIDATS.

SELECTED
BIBLIOGRAPHY

French National Politics

Association française de science politique (ed.). *Le Référendum de septembre et les élections de novembre 1958*. Paris: Armand Colin, 1960.

Barthélemy, Joseph. *Le Gouvernement de la France*. 2nd ed. Paris: Payot, 1939.

Brindillac, Charles. "Décoloniser la France," *Esprit*, XXV (December 1957), 799–812.

Buron, Robert. *Le Plus beau des métiers*. Paris: Plon, 1963.

Crozier, Michel. *The Bureaucratic Phenomenon*. Chicago: University of Chicago Press, 1964.

———. "Le Citoyen," *Esprit*, XXIX (February 1961), 193–211.

———. "La France, terre de commandement," *Esprit*, XXV (December 1957), 779–97.

Dupeux, Georges. "Le Comportement des électeurs français de 1958 à 1962," in François Goguel (ed.), *Le Référendum d'octobre et les élections de novembre 1962*. Paris: Armand Colin, 1965.

Duverger, Maurice. "The Development of Democracy in France," in Henry W. Ehrmann (ed.), *Democracy in a Changing Society*. New York: Frederick A. Praeger, 1964.

———, François Goguel, and Jean Touchard (eds.). *Les Elections du 2 janvier 1956*. Paris: Armand Colin, 1957.

Earle, Edward (ed.). *Modern France*. Princeton, N.J.: Princeton University Press, 1951.

Fauvet, Jacques. *The Cockpit of France*. London: Harvill, 1960.

———, and Henri Mendras (eds.). *Les Paysans et la politique*. Paris: Armand Colin, 1958.

Goguel, François (ed.). *Nouvelles études de sociologie électorale*. Paris: Armand Colin, 1954.

Gosnell, Harold F. *Why Europe Votes*. Chicago: University of Chicago Press, 1930.

Hoffmann, Stanley. "The Areal Division of Powers in the Writings of French Political Thinkers," in Arthur Maass (ed.), *Area and Power: A Theory of Local Government*. New York: The Free Press of Glencoe, 1959.

————, et al. *In Search of France*. Cambridge: Harvard University Press, 1965.

MacRae, Duncan, Jr., *Parliament, Parties, and Society in France, 1946–1958*. New York: St. Martin's Press, 1967.

Mead, Margaret, and Martha Wolfenstein (eds.). *Childhood in Contemporary Culture*. Chicago: University of Chicago Press, 1955.

Métraux, Rhoda, and Margaret Mead. *Themes in French Culture*. Stanford, Calif.: Stanford University Press, 1954.

Pitts, Jesse. "The Family and Peer Groups," in Norman W. Bell and Ezra F. Vogel (eds.), *A Modern Introduction to the Family*. New York: The Free Press of Glencoe, 1960.

Ridley, F., and J. Blondel. *Public Administration in France*. London: Routledge & Kegan Paul, 1964.

Siegfried, André. *France: A Study in Nationality*. New Haven: Yale University Press, 1930.

Vedel, Georges (ed.). *La Dépolitisation: mythe ou réalité?* Paris: Armand Colin, 1962.

Williams, Philip M. *Crisis and Compromise*. 3rd. ed. Hamden, Conn.: Shoe String Press, 1964.

Wright, Gordon. *Rural Revolution in France*. Stanford, Calif.: Stanford University Press, 1964.

Administrative Law and Local Finances

Bancal, Jean. *Les Circonscriptions administratives de la France*. Paris: Sirey, 1945.

Bouffard, Pierre. *Le Contrôle des délibérations du conseil municipal*. Paris: Publications Administratives, 1957.

Boulouis, Jean. *Essai sur la politique des subventions administratives*. Paris: Armand Colin, 1951.

Burdeau, Georges. *Traité de science politique*. Vol. II. Paris: Librairie Générale de Droit et de Jurisprudence, 1949.

Cathlineau, Jean. *Le Contrôle des finances communales en France*. Paris: Librairie Générale de Droit et de Jurisprudence, 1963.

Daniel, Maurice. *Les Pouvoirs de police des maires*. Paris: Librairie Technique, 1960.

Detton, Hervé. "L'Administration et la vie locale." Paris: Institut d'Etudes Politiques, 1961–62. (Mimeographed lectures.)

————. *L'Administration régionale et locale de la France.* Paris: Presses Universitaires de France, 1953.

Doueil, Pierre. *L'Administration locale à l'épreuve de la guerre.* Paris: Sirey, 1950.

"Les Finances communales," *Etude des problèmes municipaux*, No. 7 (September 1965).

France. *Code Municipal.* 1957.

————. *Financement des travaux d'équipement des collectivités locales.* Paris: Caisse des Dépôts et Consignations, 1962.

Fretin, Maurice. "L'Autonomie et la tutelle communale." Unpublished thesis. University of Paris, Faculty of Law, 1951.

Hourticq, Jean. "L'Administration et la vie locale." Paris: Institut d'Etudes Politiques, 1963–64. (Mimeographed lectures.)

Jourdan, Pierre. "La Crise de la décentralisation administrative territoriale." Unpublished thesis. University of Paris, Faculty of Law, 1954.

Lainville, Robert. *Le Budget communal.* 8th ed. Paris: Sirey, 1959.

Lelandais, Jean. *Manuel des maires, adjoints et conseillers municipaux.* Paris: Dalloz, 1949.

Maspétiol, Roland, and Pierre Laroque. *La Tutelle administrative.* Paris: Sirey, 1930.

"Les Pouvoirs de police des maires," *Etude des problèmes municipaux*, No. 10 (June 1966).

Rivero, Jean. "Le Maire, exécuteur des délibérations du conseil municipal," *Revue critique de législation et de jurisprudence*, LVII (July–October 1937), 535–605.

Roig, Charles. "Théorie et réalité de la décentralisation," *Revue française de science politique*, XVI (June 1966), 445–71.

Roy, Jacques. "L'Administration intercommunale." Unpublished thesis. University of Bordeaux, Faculty of Law, 1944.

Singer, Jean. "L'Interventionnisme communal," *Revue administrative*, XI (November–December 1958), 647–48.

————. *Le Maire et ses pouvoirs de police.* Paris: Berger-Levrault, 1959.

Tafani, Dominique. "Le Statut personnel du maire." Unpublished thesis. University of Paris, Faculty of Law, 1958.

Valentin, Lucien. *L'Action administrative dans la vie rurale.* Paris: Berger-Levrault, 1961.

Vedel, Georges. *Droit administratif.* Paris: Presses Universitaires de France, 1961.

Waline, Marcel. *Droit administratif.* Paris: Sirey, 1963.

French Community Studies

Bandet, Pierre. "L'Avenir des petites communes de la Manche." Unpublished Mémoire. Ecole Nationale d'Administration, Paris, 1958.

Beaucé, Thierry de. "Opinions et attitudes des maires ruraux." Unpublished Mémoire. Paris: Institut d'Etudes Politiques de Paris, 1964.

Beaunez, Roger. "Une Expérience où on fait confiance," *Perspectives socialistes* (January 1963).

Bernot, Lucien, and René Blancard. *Nouville, un village français*. (Travaux et Mémoires de l'Institut d'Ethnologie, LVII.) University of Paris, 1953.

Bettelheim, Charles, and Suzanne Frère. *Une ville française moyenne, Auxerre en 1950*. Paris: Armand Colin, 1951.

Clément, Pierre, and Nelly Xydias. *Vienne sur le Rhône*. Paris: Armand Colin, 1955.

Degremont, Eric. *Les Maires ruraux, leur autorité*. Paris: Institut d'Etudes Politiques de Paris, 1965.

Delarce, Jean-Jacques. "Réforme territoriale des communes." Unpublished Mémoire. Paris: Institut d'Etudes Politiques de Paris, 1962.

Josserand, Roger. "Rapport d'enquête sur la commune de Marigny en Charolais." Unpublished Mémoire. Grenoble: Institut d'Etudes Politiques de Grenoble, n.d.

Magnet, Jacques. "Les Petites communes en Charente." Unpublished Mémoire. Ecole Nationale d'Administration, Paris, 1956.

Marie, Christiane. *Grenoble 1871–1965, l'évolution du comportement politique d'une grande ville en expansion*. Paris: Armand Colin, 1966.

Mendras, Henri. *Etudes de sociologie rurale, Novis et Virgin*. Paris: Armand Colin, 1953.

Nicolay, Jean de. "Les Maires du canton de Montfort-le-Rotrou." Unpublished Mémoire. Paris: Institut d'Etudes Politiques de Paris, 1965.

Noailles, Hélie de. "Le Maire face aux problèmes communaux dans la région parisienne." Unpublished Mémoire. Paris: Institut d'Etudes Politiques de Paris, 1964.

Pitt-Rivers, Julian. "Social Class in a French Village," *The Anthropological Quarterly*, XXXIII (January 1960), 1–13.

Plaisant, François-André. "L'Avenir de la petite commune dans le Haut-Rhin." Unpublished Mémoire. Ecole Nationale d'Administration, Paris, 1958.

Rey, René. "Situation et avenir de la petite commune du Nord." Unpublished Mémoire. Ecole Nationale d'Administration, Paris, 1958.

Wylie, Laurence. *Village in the Vaucluse*. New York: Harper & Row, 1964.

———— (ed.). *Chanzeaux: A Village in Anjou*. Cambridge: Harvard University Press, 1966.

French Local Politics

Armand, Pierre-Paul. *Guide pratique de l'orateur municipal*. Paris: Publications Administratives, 1959.

Aubin, Roger. *Communes et démocratie, I: tâches et moyens de la commune; II: les communes et le pays*. Paris: Les Editions Ouvrières, 1965.

Blondel, Jean. "Local Government and the Ministries in a French Dé-

partement," Public Administration (London), XXXVII (Spring 1959), 65–74.

Brenas, Jean. "La Fonction préfectorale," *Bulletin d'information de l'association du corps préfectoral et des administrateurs civils du ministère de l'intérieur* (September 1959).

Chapman, Brian. *An Introduction to French Local Government.* London: George Allen & Unwin, 1953.

———. *The Prefects and Provincial France.* London: George Allen & Unwin, 1955.

"Demain . . . les communes," *Regards sur la France*, IX (July 1965).

Goguel, François. "Les Elections municipales des 14 et 21 mars 1965: la signification de la consultation," *Revue française de science politique*, XV (October 1965).

Gournay, Bernard. "Seminaire sur les administrations françaises." Paris: Institut d'Etudes Politiques de Paris, 1961–64. Foundation Nationale des Sciences Politiques. (Two volumes, Type-written.)

Madaule, Jacques. "Quatre ans de mairie," *Esprit*, XXI (May 1953), 768–82.

Monpied, Ernest. *Terres mouvantes, un maire rural au coeur du remembrement.* Paris: Les Editions Ouvrières, 1965.

"Municipalités et politique," *Perspectives socialistes* (January 1959).

Quereillahc, J.-L. *Un tel . . . maire.* Paris: Editions France-Empire, 1962.

Roig, Charles. "L'Administration locale et les changements sociaux," in Institut d'Etudes Politiques de Grenoble (ed.), *Administration traditionnelle et planification régionale.* Paris: Armand Colin, 1964.

Savatier, René. "La Crise et l'avenir des maires rurales," *Etudes* (March 1948), 330–46.

Schmitt, Charles. *Le Maire de la commune rurale.* Paris: Berger-Levrault, 1959.

Sharp, Walter Rice. "Local Government in France," in William Anderson (ed.), *Local Government in Europe.* New York: Appleton-Century-Crofts, 1939.

Taillandier de Gabory, Jean Claude le. "Les Conseillers généraux en Gironde depuis 1919." Unpublished Mémoire. Bordeaux: Institut d'Etudes Politiques de Bordeaux, 1959.

Taylor, Edmond. "French Politics at the Municipal Level," *The Reporter* (April 8, 1965), pp. 31–32.

Williams, Philip M. "Party, Presidency and Parish Pump," *Parliamentary Affairs*, XVIII (Summer 1965), 257–65.

Worms, Jean-Pierre. "Le Préfet et ses notables," *Sociologie du travail*, VIII (July–September 1966), 249–75.

INDEX

About the Author

MARK KESSELMAN, Assistant Professor of Government at Columbia University received his B.A. from Cornell University and his Ph.D. from the University of Chicago. He has been a Woodrow Wilson Fellow and a Falk Fellow in American Politics; he has been awarded a Fulbright Fellowship and a Social Science Research Council Predoctoral Training Fellowship to conduct research in France. Professor Kesselman has contributed articles to the *American Political Science Review* and the *Midwest Journal of Political Science.*

A Note on the Type

The text of this book is set in Electra, a typeface designed by W(illiam) A(ddison) Dwiggins for the Mergenthaler Linotype Company and first made available in 1935. Electra cannot be classified as either "modern" or "old style." It is not based on any historical model, and hence does not echo any particular period or style of type design. It avoids the extreme contrast between "thick" and "thin" elements that marks most modern faces, and is without eccentricities which catch the eye and interfere with reading. In general, Electra is a simple, readable typeface which attempts to give a feeling of fluidity, power, and speed.

W. A. Dwiggins (1880–1956) was born in Martinsville, Ohio, and studied art in Chicago. In 1904 he moved to Hingham, Massachusetts, where he built a solid reputation as a designer of advertisements and as a calligrapher. He began an association with the Mergenthaler Linotype Company in 1929, and over the next twenty-seven years designed a number of book types, of which Metro, Electra, and Caledonia have been used very widely. In 1930 Dwiggins became interested in marionettes, and through the years made many important contributions to the art of puppetry and the design of marionettes.